IMAGINING

AMERICA

IN 2033

BOOKS BY HERBERT J. GANS

The Urban Villagers: Group and Class in the Life of Italian-Americans
(Free Press, 1962; updated and expanded edition, 1982)

The Levittowners: Ways of Life and Politics in a New Suburban Community
(Pantheon Books, 1967; Columbia University Press, 1982)

People and Plans: Essays on Urban Problems and Solutions
(Basic Books, 1968)

More Equality
(Pantheon Books, 1973)

Popular Culture and High Culture: An Analysis and Evaluation of Taste
(Basic Books, 1974; revised and updated edition, Basic Books, 1999)

Deciding What's News: A Study of CBS Evening News,
NBC Nightly News, Newsweek, and Time
(Pantheon Books, 1979; 25th anniversary edition,
Northwestern University Press, 2004)

Middle American Individualism: The Future of Liberal Democracy
(Free Press, 1988; paperback, Oxford University Press, 1991)

People, Plans, and Policies: Essays on Poverty, Racism, and Other National Urban
Problems (Columbia University Press and Russell Sage Foundation, 1991)

The War Against the Poor: The Underclass and Antipoverty Policy
(Basic Books, 1995)

Making Sense of America: Sociological Analyses and Essays
(Rowman and Littlefield, 1999)

Democracy and the News
(Oxford University Press, 2003)

813.6
G157

IMAGINING AMERICA IN 2033

LIBRARY ST. MARY'S COLLEGE

HOW THE COUNTRY PUT ITSELF TOGETHER AFTER BUSH

HERBERT J. GANS

THE UNIVERSITY OF MICHIGAN PRESS

ANN ARBOR

Copyright © by Herbert J. Gans 2008

All rights reserved

Published in the United States of America by

The University of Michigan Press

Manufactured in the United States of America

♾ Printed on acid-free paper

2011   2010   2009   2008   4   3   2   1

No part of this publication may be reproduced,
stored in a retrieval system, or transmitted in any
form or by any means, electronic, mechanical, or
otherwise, without the written permission of the
publisher.

*A CIP catalog record for this book is available from
the British Library.*

Library of Congress Cataloging-in-Publication Data

Gans, Herbert J.

    Imagining America in 2033 : how the country
put itself together after Bush / Herbert J. Gans.

      p.   cm.

    ISBN-13: 978-0-472-11598-3 (acid-free paper)

    ISBN-10: 0-472-11598-7 (acid-free paper)

      1. United States—Politics and government—Fiction.

2. United States—Forecasting.   3. Twenty-first
century—Forecasts.   I. Title.

PS3607.A557I43   2008

813'.6—dc22   2008007855

A Caravan Book. For more information, visit www.caravanbooks.org.

IN MEMORY OF MARTIN MEYERSON (1922–2007),

MENTOR AND FRIEND—WHO FIRST ENCOURAGED

ME TO THINK CREATIVELY ABOUT THE FUTURE

CONTENTS

PREFACE / ix

CHAPTER ONE   2033 and Before / 1

CHAPTER TWO   Healing the Economy / 31

CHAPTER THREE   Moving toward World Peace and
                    Planetary Survival / 60

CHAPTER FOUR   Fighting for Fairness / 87

CHAPTER FIVE   Family, Home, and Community / 112

CHAPTER SIX   Schoolings / 139

CHAPTER SEVEN   Democratizing the Polity / 160

CHAPTER EIGHT   2033 and Beyond / 196

PREFACE

As the title suggests, this book is an imagined history of the first third of the twenty-first century. It describes an extraordinary period in American life in which the country put itself back together after the political and economic disasters to which it had been subjected at the start of the century. The history is selective, for it reports mainly on the major public policies of the period and the politics that help make these possible.

America in 2033 boasts a fairer economy, a more democratic polity, and institutions that cater to a greater extent to the people they are supposed to serve. Inequalities of class; race; gender; and, of course, power remain. Old problems have not disappeared, and new ones appear all the time, but American society is less polarized, its people freer from anger and paranoia and more trusting of others, including the government. For the moment even the world is nearly peaceful.

Some of the policies that have brought about the imagined better future are new, some are familiar, but they address many of the primary issues that I think will be facing America in the coming years. My history focuses especially on the period between 2012 and 2032, when most of the national rebuilding takes place.

To bring that history to life, I have imagined four presidential administrations: those of James Caruso (2012–20); Frank O'Hara (2020–24); Susan Gordon (2024–32); and Stephen Hernandez, who has spent his first year in the White House when the book ends. All but O'Hara are Democrats, although of a somewhat different stripe than now existing party leaders. That all but one is liberal reflects a hopeful opinion about the future of American liberalism. (None are intended to resemble anyone living or dead.)

For brevity's sake, I have omitted the contributions of individuals, agencies, and groups who were responsible for most of the ideas and the work for which the four leaders received or took credit. The ordinary citizens and interest groups that pressed the politicians for innovation and change and for some of the specific policies discussed here have received less than their due as well.

When all is said and done, however, and as the Bush era demonstrates once more, innovation generally is formulated from the top, by the expert and other functionaries embedded with the politicians whose values, ideas, and electoral ambitions make new programs and policies happen.

A supportive polity is also needed—one reason the history devotes a chapter to the improvement of representative democracy. And since I sought to foresee a better future, the book's polity may be more supportive, and political opposition to desirable policies more easily defeated, than in the real world. True, imagining that corporate executives and Wall Street financiers can sometimes act on their long-term interests or that they can be defeated politically may be *too* utopian. However, even they are influenced by structural changes in the society.

The structural changes that are already visible include global and national forces that will spread current reductions in job security and wages to yet other Americans, even as the prices of all forms of energy and many other necessities continue to rise.

As a result, the economy in which ordinary people live will require government help, particularly the retail economy on which so much of the overall health of the American economy now rests. Washington will have to put money in the pockets of consumers and other customers, for example by creating better jobs and other income supports for them. Indeed, the big retailers and industries that depend on them will lobby the government for such programs, pressure it to take health insurance off their shoulders, and practically force it to create a twenty-first-century welfare state.

Government will have to find the money, partly by reducing defense and other budgets. Later in the period about which I am writing government will need to complement and replace services now supplied by profit-making enterprises, look for ways of stimulating labor intensive economic growth, and levy more progressive taxes. The politicians I have imagined to be sitting in the Oval Office will not understand all the forces with which they have to cope and the structural changes that influence their policies, but they will know what they must do to hold on to their voters.

Although I write mainly about successful policies, I have included some promising ones that have so far been too impractical or unpopular to survive the political process. I include them because their time may yet come or because I wish it would come.

Conversely, the history leaves out the prosaic policies, routine politics, and customary ceremonies that always take up much of the time of the country's leading public officials. In addition, I slight the double-dealing, the backstabbing, the sexual and other affairs, the petty corruption, and the larger thefts of public funds and goods that are endemic to politics. Readers can imagine them or find them in the histories of earlier periods.

Being a sociologist and a social planner, I write with the frames and approaches of these disciplines. Sociology provides many of the analytic tools, including projection and extrapolation, but social planning offers the opportunity to predict and the freedom to imagine. Although both sometimes seek to predict the future, this book does not, instead mixing estimation, projection, and imagination. Since the history is written for general readers I have, however, kept the language free of technical qualifications and jargon.

ORIGINS

I have wanted to undertake this project for a long time. Like others of my age, I was fascinated by Edward Bellamy's utopia *Looking Back-*

ward: 2000–1887 when I was in high school, although by the time I was in college, I understood its many shortcomings. In graduate school I started thinking about someday writing what I called a realistic utopia, in which credible people, grappling with standard economic and political obstacles, were creating a better future. I was encouraged in this project by my two primary mentors, Martin Meyerson and David Riesman, both of whom were active in the post–World War II revival of interest in utopian planning.

A quarter century later, in the dark days of the Nixon years, I started to make notes for my realistic utopia. Another quarter of a century and another dark period later, I started once more and then began in earnest about the time the Supreme Court elected George W. Bush president in 2000.

The final product is not a utopia, however, because I never thought to describe a perfect and henceforth unchanging society. Nor does it quite fit the futurists' project, which emphasizes technological innovation.

Be all that as it may, I believe that imagining the future is a useful public and scholarly activity for sociology and the other social sciences—although not only for them. Every society needs to think seriously about the future and should be discussing alternative desirable futures in the appropriate policy and political arenas.

Finally, the question I was often asked when writing the book: why 2033? Originally I was going to end the story in 2050, but I could not project trends, consider the new technologies and social structures that might have appeared by then, or imagine the better society that far into the future. Once I stipulated that about a quarter century from now, the country's economy, polity, and other social structures would still resemble today's, 2033 seemed a more credible end point.

Actually, many of the changes I write about are only beginning to be implemented when my story ends, and some might take decades to come about, but remember that 2033 is an imagined date in this imagined history. Readers who are more concerned with the present should feel free to ignore 2033 and other dates, imagine the policies and politics in a contemporary setting, and think about them accordingly.

ACKNOWLEDGMENTS

Over the years many people, too many to mention, have helped with ideas and information: innumerable authors of books, reports, articles, blogs, and scripts that I read for my book, as well as friends and colleagues with whom I have talked about bits and pieces of the work.

However, I am particularly grateful to the late Peter Marris and to Frances Fox Piven, who read the entire manuscript, and to the people who commented on individual chapters: Leon Deben; Arlie Hochschild; Jeffrey Madrick; Peter Marcuse; S. M. Miller; Gary Sick; and my son, David. My wife, Louise, was as always my most demanding critic.

The book could not have been completed without the continued enthusiasm and moral support of Philip Pochoda, the director of the University of Michigan Press, who ignored the fact that it does not fit into any of publishing's established pigeonholes. Thanks also to his staff, especially those who provided twenty-first-century technical help to an author from the twentieth century: Sarah Remington; Christina Milton; Mary Bisbee-Beek; and my copy editor, Andrea Olson, whose close reading produced more clarity in my writing and fewer inconsistencies and mistakes in the narrative. I must take credit for the remaining mistakes.

New York City
October 2007

CHAPTER ONE

2033 AND BEFORE

My story begins on the evening of January 19, 2033, when a taxicab pulls up at a large but unassuming house in northwest Washington. The cab is ordinary, but its driver is a Secret Service woman, and the passengers are one past president of the United States, James Caruso (2012–20), and one outgoing president, Susan Gordon (2024–32). (The third one, Republican Frank O'Hara [2020–24], sent regrets.) The two Democrats are visiting the incoming president, Stephen Hernandez, who is to be inaugurated the next day and is spending his last free evening holed up (with one Secret Service man standing guard) in a friend's house.

That three presidential figures can be safe with one Secret Service man suggests that government officials once again believe themselves safe and that even ordinary Americans feel the country is secure. Although America is not free of enemies or domestic difficulties, it seems able to find and agree more often on effective ways to deal with them.

Like many of their meetings over the nearly twenty-five years since the three had first met, this one began stiffly. Presidents are never strong on humility, and the two visitors were now outranked by a man they still remembered as the brash twenty-two-year-old they first met in 2010. Caruso, the senior figure of the trio, was now a free floating world leader, while Gordon was just starting to think about her place in history. And both sometimes wished they were still sitting in the Oval Office.

Hernandez felt they should have given him more credit for the political first aid, fixing, and hand-holding he had supplied at various times during both Democratic administrations. He also resented the budgetary burdens his two predecessors had left for him. Still, they had worked hard to help him become president, and he would not be hosting this meeting were it not for their efforts.

Actually, the trio had worked well together despite their very different personalities. Caruso was always outgoing and cheerful even when he was depressed, while Gordon, a permanent live wire, had run for political office since she was a child. Hernandez preferred keeping quiet except when he had something to say. Although they trusted each other fully only when they were engaged in a shared task or fighting a common political enemy, they never seemed to run out of such tasks or enemies.

That Caruso was the innovator, Gordon the doer, and Hernandez the policy wonk might explain their chemistry, leading some political scientists to speculate that the country could have been put back together faster had they all been in the White House together.

The early stiffness ended after a few minutes, and the two former presidents toasted the new one. They also congratulated him for the positive state of the nation at the beginning of his term, which required him to acknowledge that if the White House deserved any credit, it should go to them. That gave Caruso, as the oldest, the opening to begin their traditional toast to the many now forgotten staffers for whose good ideas they had received credit and whose bad ones were sent back to haunt them.

Then the three began to talk about the current state of the nation, and they agreed that it had never been as together, figuratively if not literally, since the start of the century. According to the polls, most people currently believe the country is headed in the right direction, and they say that the White House and even the Congress are doing more for people like them than at any time since the question was first asked over a half century ago.

The intemperance and hostility that once polarized relations between so many people and organizations with different values and goals are much reduced. The new generations that followed the baby boomers were becoming accustomed to the changes in the family and in the organizational and political culture and even to the ups and downs of an economy that in bad times has an oversupply of workers and not enough decently paying jobs.

The stolen election of 2000 and the unnecessary war that began in 2003 and further escalated the country's political polarization have also been virtually forgotten. Red (Republican) and blue (Democratic) states have almost all become purple, except in the South. Politicians as a profession are still unlikely to win popularity polls, but they are rarely demonized or worshipped these days.

Given the fragile economy, many people need government supports and services more than in the past, one reason government is more acceptable too. In addition, the country's elected representatives are now under greater pressure to represent their voters. Swamped with citizen feedback of all kinds, they also have a better sense of what constituents need and want.

Politicians' political consciousness was raised by an activist think tank called the Democracy Project that has been urging them toward a more adequately representative democracy ever since President Caruso moved into the Oval Office. Supporters of the Project, described in detail in chapter 7, "Democratizing the Polity," claim that it has helped in creating better feelings between people and the government. Sometimes, the people even think that the government might be becoming their government.

Larger numbers vote when they can do it through the mail, while polls now ask for people's demands and other input rather than merely their opinions. Still, the politically most effective public force these days is the citizen lobbies that have grown out of various social and protest movements as well as Web-based and other mobilizations. When enough people develop new needs and demands for assistance, new citizen lobbies spring up not long after to represent them.

Like other lobbies, those representing citizens advocate for their constituencies and provide information to and exert pressure on elected and appointed officials. As a result, the corporate, professional, and other organizational lobbies no longer dominate the flow of information and influence to the Congress. That loss of influence, together with continuing advances in campaign finance reform, has cut into their power.

To be sure, the big corporations are hardly powerless, and the country remains a business-dominated society. However, the world economy is now so competitive that corporations must rely on government help more than in the past and thus must cooperate with the government nearly as often as they make demands on—or fight with—it. The once powerful business-religious alliance is ancient history now, Protestant, Catholic, Jewish, and even Muslim conservatives having become so disgusted with professional politicians that they have retreated to their churches, synagogues, and mosques. The departure of the religious conservatives from the public sphere was followed by the arrival of the seculars, who believe that the country can move forward without gods and religious politics.

Seculars have made their public appearance so recently that their actual numbers are not yet known. Even without seculars, social and economic liberals can expect to remain politically dominant when they can agree, can obtain support from the still rising number of independents, and can make the necessary compromises with centrists. Socialists remain alive, mostly on college campuses, waiting and hoping for a time when they are needed once more.

The decline in polarization and the generally upbeat public mood may also be due to the country's becoming both more alike and more equal. Regional differences are still eroding, and the continuous flow of immigrants has slowly accustomed people to having newcomers around. Most newcomers quickly accommodate themselves to the general American culture, which by now is a mix of many immigrant and older American values and practices.

Conflicts between the native born and immigrants as well as between immigrants, other than those over jobs and financial and political matters, occur less often. Now that once illegal immigrants who cannot find jobs are sent home with some spending money, nativist groups are becoming less active. White harassment of blacks and some other racial minorities is declining too, although being dark skinned remains an obstacle to public success and in everyday life.

In addition, the country is moving in the direction of greater economic equality. Very rich and very poor people remain, but there are fewer of each, and the chasms of inequality between the income groups at the top and the bottom are being filled in. As statisticians tell us, median and average income and wealth are converging and are now only a little further apart than in the western European countries that are considered the socially most civilized.

The country's rising equality is attributed to the new and often forced alliance between the domestic economy and the government. Dominated by retail and service activities, the domestic economy cannot function smoothly in the country and in the world economy without the help that only government can supply. Such help costs money, which has had to come increasingly from taxing more of the income and wealth of the most fortunate Americans. Incredible as it may seem, early in the 2020s, a Republican president had to propose a national wealth tax.

A good example of the involuntary partnership between private enterprise and government is medical care. Nearly two decades ago, the largest corporations and their business lobbies insisted that they could no longer compete in the world economy unless they were relieved of their remaining responsibilities for worker health benefits. Government had to take over these obligations quickly and therefore extended Medicare to cover practically everyone, although it had to pacify the private insurance companies that once stood in the political way by helping them find new profit-making activities.

The world economy has played a role in the country's moving toward greater equality as well. It is now clear that the United States is no longer the richest or the economically most powerful country in the world, and perhaps no single country is at the moment. In any case, as U.S. firms and entire industries become footloose, they outsource ever more of their work to countries in which labor is cheap and well trained.

As a result, the government has had to step in once more. In bad economic times especially, when jobs are scarcer, work hours are cut, and wages sometimes are reduced, the effect on people's purchasing power hurts the retail and service economies that now are so central to the overall economy. Consequently, all U.S. presidents, whether willing or not, have had to emphasize creating and saving jobs, especially those paying at least a living wage. In fact, the Democrats essentially have been driving toward a full employment economy, except that full employment no longer automatically means thirty-six to forty hours a week. Since the late 2020s, the average workweek has been moving toward thirty hours or less. If new sources of economic growth do not appear miraculously, someday the government may have to provide additional work, or income, or both.

The government's budget deficit still grows periodically. The country's financial condition would be much worse had it not been for a drastic change in foreign policy, in which the war on terror was replaced by a less expensive antiterror intelligence operation. As a result, the military and the defense budgets have shrunk significantly. Jennifer Grant, Caruso's vice president, initiated the policy change, but in retrospect, the White House had little choice. The country will no longer tolerate significant American casualties in foreign wars, and besides, Democrats are fully committed to banning unnecessary wars. If regime changes could replace other wars and civil wars around the world, more money as well as lives would be saved.

The United Nations is currently beginning to obtain the funds, know-how, and power to undertake proper peacekeeping and in the future may be able to limit the ferocity of civil and other wars. If and when the big nations feel safe enough to yield more power, the United Nations can perhaps engage in peacemaking as well. Later in the century, it may have to assemble the political power to force all nations to sharply cut their contributions to global warming.

The search for oil, oil substitutes, and cleaner fuels now preoccupies national and international leaders. Even dictatorships cannot ban cars, but vehicles have become very much smaller, including those in the United States. Gas-guzzlers are becoming museum pieces, and more Americans than ever live at higher densities. Mass transit is becoming a realistic alternative, though for most Americans, it means buses, vans, and jitneys. Still, the single family house and the lifestyle built around it remain the default ideal, federally sponsored experiments in third- to twenty-fifth-floor living notwithstanding.

The daily routines of everyday American life have remained remarkably unchanged in this century. Family forms are more varied than in the past and are expected to remain so. Even though most children are still raised by two adults, the three- to four-person nuclear family ideal has also become almost an anachronism. Voluntary childlessness has shot up; more people want the more carefree life. Singles are everywhere, and many are unattached by choice, although others spend their life seeking partners and settle down with someone in late middle or old age.

Loneliness remains a problem, yet so do family conflicts, child and partner abuse, and the passing down of dysfunctional behavior from generation to generation. New counseling projects have been created, and a national 811 hotline provides brief talking cures.

The changes in the family are found in other areas of society: old social ties are still loosening as more people choose their own. Making choices also creates problems, however. The choices are not "free," for social life is most satisfying among compatible people. Thus, loosened ties may connect the same people as before, although the ties are freer of routine obligations than in the past. For example, once people become adults and parents, they still "party" mostly with family, continuing to choose their friends among in-laws, past partners, and godparents as well as other fictive relatives. But incompatible kin may find itself frozen out.

Extrafamilial sociability continues to be found in coffee klatches, tavern cliques, clubs, and other informal groups that also function as support groups and offer their members unwitting group therapy when needed. Sometimes, the groups are adult peer groups, almost as free floating as adolescent cliques and social gangs.

Community life has become more informal too, upsetting traditionalists who mourn the decline of the visible formal organizations and voluntary associations that were once thought essential for community life and community stability. Today, people join informal groups organized around a particular goal, usually to deal with extragovernmental local problems. Most such groups begin and stay under the sociological radar, but some grow beyond their boundaries and, if often enough duplicated elsewhere, become the movements and then the citizen lobbies that today are becoming central to representative democracy.

Education has taken on a more central role than in the past, even though work time shrinkage and the possibly permanent reduction in the number of high skill professional jobs are now raising questions about how much education is actually needed. The greater emphasis on education began with a federal small classes program that was instituted to create more jobs. Then, a good deal of experimentation took place to increase the involvement of young people in their own education, including having them teach each other.

Political education has been the most dramatic curriculum innovation. High school students now learn to understand how politics works in the country, in their communities, and even in their schools, although the courses, the research projects, and the workshops came into being only after a protracted struggle with many very nervous local school boards. Another generation will have to go by before the effects of these courses on the country's political life can be evaluated.

As of now, electoral politics has not changed much, even though a majority of the voters have graduated college. Most people still are driven largely by self-interest and family interests—and these interests also explain the few occasions when most participate in community and national political life. Politics itself remains largely an elite and specialist domain, and the players' drives for power and money still compete with the values they bring with them into the political game.

Raw greed may have declined a bit, but maybe the greedy are only holding their fire till a supportive government is in power again. National crime rates have been declining almost continually, except in the worst economic times, but that may reflect the boost in equality over the last couple of decades.

However, people who might be in jail had they not helped to write the laws that legitimate their action still get into the halls of power. Petty corruption, corner cutting, and the constant competition and struggling for personal advantage have not disappeared in the White House or elsewhere. Presidents hand out a lot of medals and issue proclamations for altruistic acts, but self-interested agendas continue to lurk behind people's worthy contributions. Many good people have worked hard for the policies that have improved American life over the last two decades, but none have turned into angels.

Remembrances

The final part of the evening was devoted to fondly remembered policy innovations and political moments. Caruso spoke most passionately about his job creation innovations and about bringing "tender loving care" to medical care through the nurse-doctors, nurses also trained as primary care physicians. He reminded his colleagues of the political virtues of exploiting splits in the business community, one of the methods that he had used to obtain the economic policies that benefited Americans earning less than the median income and took credit for first suggesting a tax on obscene profits.

Gordon spoke proudly about inventing the Earned Estate Tax Credit that enabled all Americans to leave at least a small estate to their children and about getting Congress to approve an adequate wealth tax. However, she was proudest about eliminating the government's ability to launch unnecessary wars. Hernandez was most pleased with the courses in practical politics that he introduced into public education while he served as Caruso's Secretary of Education.

All three enjoyed once more the thought of a Republican president having to propose the first wealth tax to pay the federal bills, but Gordon also remembered the hard political work to get Americans to drive more slowly to reduce carbon emissions.

The three leaders no longer remembered who first decided that the Constitution could be amended to make the country more democratic but said they would be pleased that Hernandez would receive the historical credit if the amendments were approved during his time in the White House.

Finally, the president-elect reminded his two guests that they all had to get a few hours of sleep, and Caruso got up to offer another toast that they repeated whenever they met as a trio. Once more, they expressed their appreciation to George W. Bush and his team, noting again that probably none of them would be where they were today had Bush not been so effective at nearly ruining the country.

THE THREE PRESIDENTS

The three presidents had first met in early December 2010. The occasion was a weekend conference at a small family foundation devoted to liberal activism that had recently joined a network of other foundations, think tanks, and activist groups. This network called itself the Tiny Liberal Conspiracy (TLC) and would one day give birth to the Democracy Project.

The purpose of the conference was to try to figure out yet once more how liberals and centrists could come together so that the Democrats could win the 2012 election. Caruso had been invited to give the keynote address. He and Gordon already knew each other from other think tank gatherings as well as Democratic party meetings, and both were struggling with how to leave the liberals in charge if and when the two major party factions were brought together.

Afterward the two went to dinner together. Later, Hernandez, then a program assistant at the foundation, came over to their table to introduce himself and was invited to join them. At 3 a.m. the restaurant manager asked them to leave so she could close the place.

James Caruso

In 2010, Jim (James) Caruso, now forty-eight, had already spent over a quarter century in California Democratic politics and, as he sometimes liked to say, many of the previous years thinking about how to become president. A month before the foundation conference, he had briefly appeared in the national spotlight because of his landslide reelection in one of the reddest congressional districts in the state.

After Caruso had made the rounds of the political talk shows and had been written about in the major political blogs, an astonishing number of politicians, voters, and people who identified themselves as reformed nonvoters suggested that he should think about running for the presidency. At first he dismissed them, arguing that he was a mere congressman, but his new fans said the country needed a politician who was closer to the people than his predecessors. Initially Caruso was also sure that it was already too late to initiate a campaign, but in January 2013, slightly over two years later, he moved into the Oval Office.

In his youth, Caruso had really hoped to become an actor, although later he decided that being a politician was a fine substitute. He enjoyed playing the variety of roles necessary to the job and realized that becoming a star was easier in the hierarchical world of politics than in the relatively egalitarian one of entertainment. He also liked to use his thespian rhetorical tricks in debates, although he was always more eager to win over his audience than his opponent.

Caruso's genuine friendliness was backed up by an equally genuine toughness. He had played political hardball when necessary and with only a modicum of guilt, and he secretly admired the political genius that led Karl Rove, Dick Cheney, and George W. Bush to try to turn the country into a permanent one party state. True, he was appalled by their goals and could not stomach their methods, but he knew that the Democrats would have to craft their own kind of party loyalty in order to earn enough time to turn the country into a healthy democracy.

Although he grew up in California, Caruso was actually a descendant of an old western Massachusetts working class family. His father had been an electrician who was active in party politics after hours. His mother was an assistant to a social worker, and as a youngster, Caruso thought he would become a social worker. In college, he discovered acting, journalism, and politics, but after a frustrating year spent trying to break into the movies, he began his working life driving a truck and stringing cable for what was then still the phone company. A year later, however, he was a fledgling political reporter in southern California. Subsequently, he moved to northern California to handle political communications for San Jose's mayor and not long afterward became her political adviser.

Then, Caruso ran for the state house, serving two terms in the California Senate until he became lieutenant governor and, for a while, actually ran the state for the governor. The college leading man became a stellar performer on the campaign trail, and the former reporter knew how to get the journalists to cover him. In fact, the first time he had seriously thought about the presidency occurred when a political opponent in Sacramento told him that he was good enough at grandstanding to become the leader of the free world.

However, underneath all his political skins, Caruso was also a dreamer who wanted to be remembered in history for creating a fairer America. As the first in the family to go to college, he had seen his relatives endure difficult economic times and harsh treatment by the organizations and individuals that ultimately controlled their fate. College had helped him to understand how widely his family's place in society diverged from that of his affluent fellow students. Later, he automatically remembered his college days whenever he met the elites who dominated national politics.

Two of Caruso's political dreams were actually closer to obsessions. One, based on his ancestors' job troubles, was his desire to provide full-time work at decent pay for everyone seeking work; the other was making representative democracy work properly. He thought these two goals were related. Once he started campaigning for the presidency, he understood that he would have to reward or fight the business community to obtain full employment and to reform representative democracy so that he could obtain citizen support for this struggle.

Caruso's vice presidential choice, Jennifer Grant, came with a totally different background. Born into a southern military and political family, she had never run for political office but was a West Point graduate who had served in Iraq, the Pentagon, and the U.S. Department of State. When Caruso asked her to become his vice president, she was a UN executive with relief and peacekeeping responsibilities. A little older than Caruso, she was more conservative economically, which pleased the centrists, but she was liberal on the social issues that appealed to the party's more affluent voters. More important, Grant was well versed in defense and foreign policy and was already scheduled to take them over in the White House if Caruso won the election.

Caruso's wife, Rose Brown Caruso, came from a somewhat more bourgeois background She grew up in Ohio, and many people believed she was the Caruso camp's top political strategist. The couple's three children were all young adults, but they regularly appeared in the White House for family dinners, some of which were large enough to be described as tribal gatherings by cynical or envious White House staffers.

Susan Gordon

In 2024, Susan Gordon entered the record books as the first single woman in American history to run successfully for the presidency. Although never an active feminist, she thought that women should have run for the presidency as soon as they won the right to vote. Today, however, the country's demand for inspired and skillful leadership is so urgent that the candidates' gender—and race, religion, and other personal attributes—has become irrelevant.

Gordon grew up in Florida, the only child of two lawyers, her mother a public defender. Rumor had it that her ancestors came to the Lower East Side of New York as Goldbergs and became Gordons when they moved south. She never affirmed or denied the story and in effect turned her name into a projective test onto which members of the public projected their own beliefs about her origins. Her silence helped her particularly among voters of Scotch Irish and Irish origin—or at least those who still knew the origins of their immigrant ancestors—who thought she was one of theirs.

Gordon was thirty-seven when Caruso won the 2012 election, but she showed up early in politics, enjoying a short but exciting career in Florida public school and college politics and managing a State House campaign for an ex-boyfriend before she graduated from law school. She ran against him in the next election and spent two additional terms in the state legislature. Then she was elected to Congress, where she first met Caruso. She played a vital behind the scenes role in his first and second presidential campaigns, but in 2016, she ran successfully for governor of Florida and in 2020 was elected to a second term. Actually, she wanted to go for the presidency that year but yielded, not entirely graciously, to Jennifer Grant.

Gordon had in fact never completely left the national political scene in all the years she was immersed in Florida politics. Caruso, Grant, and many other Democratic politicians relied on her for her uncanny ability to sense whether the country was ready for innovative policies and new ideas. She always seemed to know just how far the political envelope could be pushed and thus was particularly useful to progressive Democratic politicians all over the country. They then returned the favor when she set out for the White House.

Gordon's political skills were supplemented by a perky, almost adolescent extroversion. She was a superb organizer who could get people to work at the most unrewarding tasks, and she was also a persuasive negotiator. Caruso once told her that she probably could have negotiated a compromise on environmental legislation between vice president and oil company executive Dick Cheney and Ralph Nader, a founder of the American Green party. She saw herself as a doer, and she actually spent much of her time in the Oval Office advancing or completing what Caruso had initiated.

Although Gordon never gave much explicit thought to her political values, she had developed her own version of the Caruso principles and at least some of his empathy with underdogs. She never knew where that empathy originated, not having ever lived with underdogs. Besides, she thought that her pervasive knowledge of how to deal with overdogs would be useful for helping the underdogs.

Because Caruso was male, gender had been an issue of little consequence to him during his campaign, but Gordon had first campaigned as a woman—and a Democrat—when, not long after puberty, she won the presidency of her seventh grade class. She broke a number of glass ceilings during her ascent to the White House and shattered further ones from the Oval Office. But she also looked out for the men who were bearing the brunt of a shrinking labor market.

Gordon was proud, too, to be the first single president in the White House and thereby to represent the still rising number of unmarried individuals in the country. Her emotional life was, however, devoted to politics and to the people she associated with as a result of that passion. Unlike Caruso, she enjoyed nearly everything about politics, as if it were a drug to which she was addicted. Her enjoyment was almost physical; she loved being in the middle of the action, and once she embarked on her campaign for president, she dreaded the isolation that sometimes came with the presidency.

Gordon had been in her share of relationships before she entered Democratic politics and maintained occasional contact with three of them—"friends with benefits," they were called when she was young. They were far removed from politics, and she could let her hair down with them, but while she was president she always wondered what would happen if they suddenly made the headlines. However, several of the women who were suddenly elevated to important positions all over Washington when Gordon was elected had made similar arrangements.

Gordon had picked her vice president, General Richard Potter, even before she decided to run for the presidency. He was an old friend from the Midwest, though one without benefits, and Gordon had met him when he was a young one-star general in Iraq. Angered by the useless bloodshed on all sides, he requested reassignment, knowing it would end his career, and he resigned after a year as a Pentagon strategic planner.

Too taciturn to be a politician but a crackerjack administrator, Potter first worked for the World Bank, but when Gordon met him he was back in frontline action running an international non-governmental organization (NGO) struggling to eradicate AIDS. Like Caruso's Grant, he served Gordon as the de facto president in charge of foreign affairs, and though by then he was virtually a pacifist, he could have functioned as a shadow commander in chief had it been necessary.

Stephen Hernandez

Steve Hernandez, the grandson of a Mexican migrant worker, originally wanted to be a high school teacher but even in community college found that his peers looked to him for guidance. That discovery, in addition to his energy level and his restlessness, made it plain that his abilities lent themselves more to politics than teaching. He finished up at a selective college and then spent two years teaching junior high school in one of New York's barrios, which stimulated his lifelong passion for educational reform. However, his history and experience made him a natural token Latino, and in 2010 he was working at the New York foundation where he met Caruso and Gordon.

After Caruso was elected, he offered Hernandez a White House staff position, and for the next several years, Hernandez was Caruso's point man on education. In 2016, he was named Caruso's Secretary of Education, the youngest person ever to hold that post. He also became active in national Latino politics, often brokering among and between the West and East Coast Latino politicians.

In 2020 he became president of a major national foundation where, he later said, he could meddle further in education. He ran successfully for governor of New Mexico in 2024, was reelected in 2028, and became president of the United States in 2032. At times during his rise to the political top, he thought he was still the token Latino, but in fact he served as a role model for what social scientists describe as the "deracialization" or "whitening" of Latino Americans. Privately, however, he prided himself on being an immigrant kid living in the White House.

Hernandez's personality was almost a total opposite of Caruso's and Gordon's. Because he was essentially a private and quiet man, his public appearances were naturally low key. That seemed to make his political audiences feel comfortable, which only made him more electable.

However, Hernandez had the same social advantage as Caruso: he was middle class enough to be mainstream—and also to attract the better off Latinos who might have thought of going Republican—but he could effortlessly demonstrate his family's lowly origins to the less well off. Perhaps because he was so low key, he was rarely threatening to Anglos, including those worried about the alleged Latinization of America.

Low key or not, Hernandez was very good at governing, in some respects far better than Caruso or Gordon, as they realized whenever they sought his advice. His eagerness to find the best policies to achieve public and political goals was partly responsible; as a result, he was often described as a lovable policy wonk, ideal for meeting the challenges that would face America in the 2030s.

Hernandez was also more a do-gooder than his two Democratic predecessors, and he never lost his interest in educational reform. Convinced that kids, especially poor ones, learned best by being involved in their own schooling, he looked for ways to involve them. Educators who objected were pacified by Hernandez's equally strong conviction that the school had to be good enough for the youngsters to become involved.

During his tenure as president Caruso had stressed the importance of a "fair" America, and Hernandez liked that concept, although Hernandez was more ruled by egalitarian principles than Caruso, principles reinforced by some guilt over his own upward mobility. He also never quite gave up the fear that his success would end someday, leaving him little better than a migrant worker in his old age. Awareness that the guilt and the fear were irrational only drove him more toward egalitarianism even when it was politically risky.

In addition, Hernandez benefited from his wife, Elizabeth, on those occasions when he could inveigle her to participate in his campaign events. Elizabeth was a doctor who had moved into public health about the time her husband entered politics, and she liked to warm up Hernandez's political meetings by dispensing medical advice. Born in New York, she described herself as having so many different ancestors that she could be a member of nearly every ethnic and racial organization in the country. She took special pride in a black great-grandfather and introduced herself as multi-multiracial in the parts of the country in which a visible multiracial constituency was emerging.

Hernandez found his vice president in Shirley Johnson, who fit most of the stereotypes that had been piled on America's heartland but who actually had been born in New Jersey. Married to a former senator, she had served as an ambassador in several countries. However, she later had returned to school and received a PhD in environmental chemistry. Hernandez depended on her for her knowledge of finance, foreign affairs, and global warming issues.

AMERICA IN 2010

In 2010, the United States was often described as a chronically ill country just beginning to admit it was very sick. The corporate economy was the first to complain: profits were declining virtually across the board. Employees had been grumbling for years about flat wages and salaries, but now more and more were doing so openly. Even official joblessness was rising, and discouraged workers were further depressing the labor force participation rate, thereby raising the de facto unemployment rate to western European levels.

Some new jobs still paid well, very well in fact, but only some. A growing number of college graduates ended up taking jobs away from high school graduates, and in many places, the jobs for the latter paid so little that they were advertised mainly in immigrant neighborhoods. The gap between population growth and job creation was widening, and economists were speculating that this trend would continue for the foreseeable future. Some historians even claimed that modern economies had always suffered from an excess of workers, except in wartime. Only productivity was still heading upward, thanks in part to management speedups and the continuing replacement of workers by robots.

Many observers ascribed the open grumbling to the increasing inroads on job security. More buyouts and lengthening layoffs suggested that the de facto tenure many corporate white collar workers had long enjoyed was ending even as health insurance contributions and pensions continued to shrink. Moreover, the keepers of the conventional economic wisdom had finally realized that economic insecurity led to a host of stress-related illnesses and social problems, from depression, cardiac diseases, and addictions to child abuse, spouse battering, and of course street crime.

Some sectors of the economy continued to be innovative, and others rose to the challenge as more former third world countries, particularly in Asia, now had money to spend. The year 2010's strongest boom was the comfort sector, so named because it exported goods and services that helped make everyday life more comfortable for affluent Asians.

Unfortunately, however, innovations now enjoyed only brief staying power; everything could be copied quickly and more cheaply by other countries all over the world. Consequently, development economists who looked ahead were already asking what role America would play in the world economy once other countries could invent the goods and services that had always originated here. Fortunately, all countries needed foreign customers for the goods and services they produced and soon overproduced; consequently they would always have to import some of what America was selling. Still, pessimists thought that someday Americans would be hired to make cheap copies of foreign inventions.

The good news was that the patient had finally received some attention from the political establishment. Moderates from both parties had forced some tax loophole closings and the revocation of Bush tax cuts that had not yet expired. Defense spending was being reduced slightly for the first time in many years. Although the Pentagon was still trying to end the killing in Iraq and elsewhere, its attempt to impose Republican forms of capitalism and representative democracy on the Middle East was over. The moderates had also pushed through at least a temporary halt to some costly new weapons development.

The Political Scene in 2010

Nevertheless, the country's polity was as turbulent as the economy. The George W. Bush administration's fanaticism, incompetence, and corruption had both eroded the legitimacy of the White House and increased the demand for candidates without skeletons in their closets. Congress was hampered by the divisions in both major parties and the ever rising numbers of poll respondents who identified themselves as independents. In fact, some analysts were beginning to distinguish between Democratic and Republican independents, and various hopefuls were testing third party waters.

On the Republican side, pre-Bush moderates retrieved some of their past influence while the declining group of conservatives began to break apart. The religious conservatives were ready to declare war against the economic conservatives, and reporters interviewed middle income evangelicals who could not pay their bills and said they would have to vote Democratic in 2012. Even the Republican party leadership could not persuade the business conservatives to support legislation that would help their religious fellow Republicans to avoid going broke.

The religious leadership itself had split. The media stars continued to preach the Rapture or the GOP gospel, but the pastors who had to serve and service their flocks were having to deal with budget problems. Although they continued to oppose abortion and the other so-called sex issues, they were busy trying to pay for popular but expensive social services that local governments had stopped supplying even as economically troubled worshippers reduced their donations.

The economic conservatives were fighting too. The corporations selling retail goods and services in the domestic economy called for increases in the public's purchasing power, while those competing with overseas firms, the financial industry, and others advocated further cuts in taxes and domestic spending.

Republican foreign policy was paralyzed. The remaining planners of worldwide Texas-style democracy had departed, often involuntarily, after which many of their former allies returned to the GOP's traditional isolationism without much ideological qualm.

Without a solid party behind them, the party professionals could not use the strategies that had immobilized Democratic candidates and had helped the GOP win so many elections. Only the Republican ideologues still stood comparatively fast. Although the old squabbles between the several Far Right factions continued, the foundations that saturated the elite and the media with publications, videos, blogs, and Web sites papered over their ideological differences and continued to function.

So did right-wing talk shows, news programs, columnists, and bloggers, but some of the biggest names were losing audiences and credibility. A few liberal and centrist think tanks were even rattling the conservatives with some of their own techniques. As a result, the conservative arguments became shriller, which further impaired their credibility. For example, fiery demands for protecting the national interest in the Middle East turned off young people who had seen too many of their friends come back from the wars with physical or mental injuries.

The Democrats were more fortunate, being split only between centrists and liberals and coming together more often to take advantage of the Republican chaos. Still, the widening gaps in the GOP impacted them as well. Some centrists were being wooed by Republican moderates to form a bipartisan caucus, and the social liberals continued to fight with the economic ones. The former also went shopping for support among moderate Republicans, while the latter were still trying to figure out what economic programs for the low and moderate income population the affluent middle class, Democratic or independent, would support.

Liberals who were normally hesitant to appear anticapitalist joined the Left Liberals in calling for a twenty-first-century great society modeled on the twentieth-century Scandinavian welfare state. Outside observers thought the liberals would do best by supporting whatever Democratic politicians possessed enough power and resources to bang heads together.

Judging by the polls, many voters were alternatively resigned and angry, the anger surfacing when economic conditions deteriorated close to home: when unemployment, the price of gasoline, the cost of heating oil or coal, food prices, and housing expenses rose at the same time. Their economic fear was driving away fears directed at terrorists and other foreign and domestic devils.

As a result, optimists thought they could see changes coming in political life. Political Web sites that still appealed mainly to upper middle class liberals and enthusiastic college students were now receiving responses and donations from middle America. Popular video Web sites were showing a constantly increasing number of videos with political and economic complaints and appeals.

Hard-boiled political operatives were skeptical that Web-based enthusiasm would translate into more than symbolic or media politics. Meanwhile, their more hopeful peers were searching for the organizational and other techniques that would get more of the Web constituencies to the polls in 2012. That would first mean attracting and holding their attention during the long primary and election campaigns and the candidates' petty squabbling to garner media attention.

The politically hopeful were also calling on new Web-based organizations advocating in behalf of young parents, singles, homeowners, drivers with rising fuel bills they could not afford, and the chronically ill, among others. Some of these organizations would give rise to parallel social movements, and later some of them transformed themselves into the first of the new citizen lobbies. These citizens lobbies represented and advocated in behalf of ordinary people rather than the corporations and other formal organizations, as well as the professionals and similar elites, that had always paid for most of the lobbying taking place in Washington.

A few social democratic and democratic socialist parties revived in big cities and college towns, including in the redder parts of the country. (Rumor had it that some Republicans then demanded a color change in the national political map.) The parties were tiny and conflict ridden, but their blogs were closely followed in Washington by major party operatives looking for policy ideas. But then everyone inside the Beltway seemed to spend their spare time writing or reading blogs.

HOW IT ALL GOT STARTED; THE FIRST CARUSO CAMPAIGN

In spring 2011, Jim Caruso began to move in earnest toward his run for the presidency. The year 2011, he realized, was normally already too late to start campaigning, but for once coming in behind the pack might hold some advantages. The two major parties had produced familiar and predictable candidates who became even more familiar and predictable during the long campaign. Caruso thought that a newcomer would be helped by avoiding media and voter stereotypes of—as well as boredom with—them. A new face somewhat later in the game might pique new curiosity. His ties to the political Web community together with the right messages and the resulting media coverage could even reduce his dependency on the most demanding campaign funders.

In addition, Caruso promised to refrain from the daily exchange of charges that consumed most election campaigns but that many voters neither could nor would follow. Instead, he would offer a domestic or foreign policy proposal or another new idea at least once a week, just in time for the Sunday talk shows and the Monday morning newspaper and Web site headlines.

As expected, Caruso's campaign concentrated on the economy, foreign affairs, and the redemocratization of America. He liked to start his economic stump speeches by describing the economy as a juggling act involving four balls: the usually healthy profit economy; the salary economy, where the best jobs could be found; the wage economy, which often had more workers than jobs; and the garbage economy of underpaid jobs and inadequate benefits. The juggling act metaphor often ended up in disparaging footnotes in neoclassical economics textbooks, but Caruso's audiences cheered, because it described the economy in which they were living. They cheered even more when he added that none of the balls should have to drop but that he would work hardest for those now in the wage and garbage economies.

Strengthening the wage economy was particularly necessary because it employed so many people. Caruso talked a lot about the below median income Americans who occupied the lower half of the wage economy. He also described them as the working people, thereby setting himself off from his rivals, many of whom spoke for a middle class that sometimes included only the top 10 percent of the income distribution.

Whenever it was relevant to do so, Caruso would gingerly debunk what he thought was a sometimes unnecessary adversarial dichotomy between government and private enterprise. To those parts of the business community that depended on government programs supporting their customers, suppliers, or workers he pointed out that their interests differed from those of other parts of that community, especially those who were interested only in yet lower taxes, less regulation, and more privatizing of government.

Actually, Caruso developed these ideas into a strategy: woo the corporations that need you, fight the others, and when possible create splits between kinds of firms. To the former, he offered a deal: the government will assist you to grow, but you must help pay the bill in corporate and other taxes as well as with decent treatment of workers and their unions. The strategy did not always work, and the business community continued to let ideology trump its economic interests more than everyone else.

Caruso promised the unions that he would seek to return the rights they had lost since World War II, but he urged service workers with space-bound jobs that could not be outsourced to join international unions, which could threaten to call global general strikes. Others he bade think harder about what kinds of worker representatives were suitable for the twenty-first-century service and knowledge economy. He spoke favorably about white collar worker associations and the associations of teachers and other salaried professionals, but eventually he came to realize that at least until the unions were fully back on their feet, they should be complemented by employee lobbies.

Caruso said little further about domestic policy, but he promised to try to end the conservative dominance in the federal courts. Privately, he was unsure about how to do it, but he considered generous buyouts of older judges as well as unending White House and congressional pressure to follow the election returns. Congress could regularly pass new legislation to moot or reverse Supreme Court decisions, and perhaps government in general could constantly question conservative decisions.

Caruso down played foreign policy but instead emphasized defense policy. He would end the fearmongering associated with the war on terror, relying instead on a broad-based international hunt for actual terrorists, the people who terrorized and attacked innocent civilians. Hunts were less likely to kill innocent civilians than wars, and they would be much cheaper as well. He then distinguished between terrorists and participants in civil or postcolonial wars, suggesting that the latter were terrorists only when they were killing civilians. Policing civil and postcolonial wars should eventually become the responsibility of the United Nations, and Caruso favored strengthening the United Nations for this purpose as quickly as possible.

As Caruso and his advisers expected, his terrorism speech resulted in a barrage of accusations from some of his primary opponents as well as most Republicans. However, the initial poll reactions were favorable, and so he continued to give the speech. Ignoring the attacks on him was not easy, but he received political and emotional support from many political Web sites.

In his redemocratization stump speech, Caruso pleaded for a representative democracy in which every person had one vote and no groups or individuals could buy others, even if that took some constitutional amendments. Like others, he inveighed against arbitrary redistricting and gerrymanders and proposed the abolition of the Electoral College. Every so often, he spoke about needing an ideologically balanced Supreme Court and other federal courts. He asked for judges that would respect legislation necessary to undo the damage done to government and the economy by Ronald Reagan and his Republican successors.

Caruso also offered some immediately achievable ideas about how to bring government closer to the citizenry, and some he tried out at once. Among other things, he asked people to submit policy ideas for the Caruso administration, and the campaign nearly went broke processing the flood of e-mails and letters that followed.

Then, Caruso announced that his cabinet would not be limited to former bankers, corporation executives, and high priced lawyers. He would also find people who formerly had been working people or had served them. His Secretary of Labor would have put in time on an assembly line or as a computer programmer, the Secretary of Defense would have served in the military as an enlisted man or woman, and the attorney general might well be a former public defender.

Later, he announced the names of and campaigned with some of the people he said he would appoint to the cabinet if he became president so that the voters would get to know the people who would do much of the heavy lifting if he were elected. Campaigning with them allowed Caruso to test them in the hand-to-hand combat of political life; on their ability to work with him; and, as a couple of them found out to their dismay, on their skill in outcampaigning their boss.

Caruso campaigned most intensely with his press secretary to be, who could thus begin working with journalists who would later be covering the president. Meanwhile, she would become a familiar figure among the voters following the campaign, who, if Caruso became president, would see her nearly every day when she briefed the news media.

Caruso actually wanted to name his vice president before the beginning of his primary campaign but was persuaded to hold off. He did, however, announce that he would name a woman, someone with enough foreign policy experience to oversee the administration's overseas activities and the domestic activities that impacted them. He knew whom he wanted to nominate and let the journalists start a guessing game, which quickly spread to the celebrity magazines, thus publicizing the Caruso campaign to the millions of hard-to-reach young people who kept up with these media.

Over the course of the campaign Caruso spoke about other issues, many of which are reported in later chapters of this book. In addition, he constantly looked for opportunities to portray himself as a social moderate. For example, he hoped that if any of his children were gay, they would be monogamous and have the opportunity to marry. He supported what he called bodily choice but hoped abortions would not take place after the first trimester. At the same time, he questioned conventional priorities, believing obesity to be a bigger problem than illegitimacy.

He described himself as a believing Catholic who tried to practice his religion in places other than in the church. He also presented himself as a faithful environmentalist when people's health was at stake but as being in favor of job creation over saving an endangered minor species. He was frightened by global warming and its effects on the lives of his children and grandchildren, and he announced that fossil fuel and energy consumption would have to begin declining in earnest.

Twice Caruso interrupted his election campaigning to discuss global warming with international experts and world leaders, but his campaign benefited most from a promise by several of the leaders to join him in reducing the use of coal until economically viable antipollution technology became available. The promise contained enough loopholes not to panic American coal producers, but Caruso also promised them more federal assistance for carbon cleaning and disposal research.

In retrospect, Caruso won the primaries and received the nomination mainly because he was sufficiently different from his opponents. For decades, most of the top Democratic politicians came from elite backgrounds or had achieved elite positions before running for the presidency—and Caruso had not. Ultimately, having served as a lowly congressman helped him too.

However, his social and economic background helped even more, for his family's working class origins made him simpatico especially among people who were worried that they and their children might never move up into the middle class. He attracted young people by reminding them that he had begun his education at a community college and that he had never even given a speech at any of the Ivy League schools.

As an actor, Caruso could speak upper and upper middle class English when the situation demanded it, but even on such occasions he found a way to remind people of his class origin. He could sound and be presidential when required, and if necessary, he even took on the bullying tone that had once helped George W. Bush capture the votes of angry and scared Americans. In 2012, however, he needed to speak with a reassuring voice and to avoid the adversarial rhetoric that marked most elections.

He kept his distance from the writers, intellectuals, celebrities, and rich do-gooders who usually gravitated to Democratic politicians. Normally, he enjoyed talking to most of them, but he knew that many voters distrusted them. Too many of them flaunted their high status, even if not intentionally. They often failed to see that their faith in the universality of their social and cultural values appeared arrogant to people with different values. Sometimes Caruso tried to tell them that the more populist their talk, the more off-putting they could sound.

The politically astute intellectuals understood what Caruso was saying, but others were unhappy about being left out. They liked his economic policies but could not understand why he was conservative on some social issues. He made them uncomfortable in other ways, as they him, and they looked nostalgically to the 1960s, when the Kennedy family, who some claimed had been genuine intellectuals, dominated the Democratic party.

Once elected, Caruso brought the intellectuals who understood what he was doing and who could help him into his government. By that time, however, he had filled many visible positions in his government with people who had originally come from working class and lower middle class backgrounds. At times, Caruso liked to brag that he ran a government of common people.

Caruso did not call attention to his own ethnicity until the Republicans resorted once more to swifting. A group claiming to be crime fighters charged that Caruso's immigrant ancestors had been involved with the Mafia. Even before the campaign had a chance to respond, Italian Americans from all parts of the country who had not thought about their ancestry for years erupted in fury. The backlash hurt the GOP so badly that it virtually ended swifting, although some Democrats were sorry that they now might never get to try swifting the Republicans.

THE CARUSO VICTORY

Caruso's victory in November 2012 was not purely his own. In some states, he ran on the coattails of popular incumbent Democrats; in others, he won because many people were voting against Republicans. He leaned heavily on Gordon and Hernandez but had help from two unexpected spark plugs.

One of these spark plugs was the already mentioned set of think tanks and activists who called themselves the TLCs. The major contribution to the campaign was a group of young volunteers who dreamed up new campaign ideas when the staffers responsible for the day-to-day campaign started to burn out from overwork. Later, they formed the nucleus of an informal White House brainstorming task force that then set up branches in every major government agency. They also persuaded Caruso to set up a new organization, the Council of Long-Range Advisers, to complement the already established Council of Economic Advisers and Council of Social Advisers.

The other spark was contributed by Caruso's running mate, Jennifer Grant, who brought ideological and gender balance and foreign affairs expertise to the campaign. More important, she somehow turned Caruso and herself into a pair that played well off each other when they campaigned together.

Like Caruso, Grant enjoyed arguing, and one very warm Friday midway in the campaign, the two did so in public. Grant had made a speech about how the administration would deal with future terrorist attacks should they occur, and Caruso, who was not entirely happy with her speech, suggested they discuss the subject further.

The discussion played so well in the media that they found time for several more. The most popular one concerned their experience disciplining unruly children, with not a word of politics spoken during the entire time.

Caruso's and Grant's conversation about race evoked a particularly lively audience reaction. One day, Grant announced that like most white southerners, she undoubtedly had some black ancestors. The announcement had been planned in advance, but she presented it so matter of factly that as the exit polls later showed, her remarks alienated only a few southern whites. However, it also brought enough new black voters to help Caruso carry a couple of states that normally voted Republican.

True, the Democrats had already overcome many of the party's long-standing electoral difficulties with race. However, "race mixing" had not come up before, and some party leaders feared that the Republicans would revive that once explosive issue with negative advertising. Caruso compensated for these fears by enlisting Hernandez to campaign for a larger Latino turnout. The increasing visibility of multiracial figures in leadership positions helped too, although white anxiety and hostility toward African Americans remained evident, and not just in the South.

The Caruso-Grant conversation about race and its electoral payoff led to today's practice of all candidates submitting their DNA tests along with their tax returns. Although the experts keep insisting on the limited validity of the tests, since the 2020s, the results have enabled politicians to demonstrate that they are all racial and ethnic hybrids.

Studies conducted after the 2012 election indicated the effectiveness of what inevitably became the Caruso-Grant show, and the two leaders continued their discussions nearly every weekend for the next eight years. People enjoyed the warmth the two politicians displayed for each other when they disagreed, and their occasional misstatements and subsequent retractions went over well. The voters liked their politicians behaving as ordinary humans, and over the years campaign language became a little more like everyday conversation.

In fact, the Caruso-Grant show attracted more viewers than the campaign's political advertising and the presidential and vice presidential debates, which then were still largely exchanges of stump speech excerpts. In later years, the advocates of public campaign financing used the success of the show as one argument to reduce the amount of traditional campaign advertising.

As most commentators had predicted, Caruso's victory margin was tiny, but the Democrats controlled the Congress. The liberals outnumbered the centrists, if only barely, but the opposition lacked enough votes to override Caruso's vetoes. Still, Caruso would have to fight for every item on his agenda.

As it turned out, Caruso's Democratic successors faced the same challenge. Although all dreamed of a liberal-dominated Congress, either the House or the Senate always had a sizable centrist caucus that would often be joined by the more conservative independents and even some moderate Republicans. As a result, the Congress almost always slowed down the White House's liberal initiatives, thereby pleasing the still numerous voters who were most comfortable with a divided federal government.

After the election, the pollsters suggested that the Republicans deserved some credit for Caruso's victory. The GOP had attempted to win the election by wooing enough independents and unhappy Democratic centrists to what was left of their traditional base. As a result, the party was forced to balance an ideologically unyielding conservative presidential candidate with a moderate vice presidential running mate, but their discomfort with each other was apparent to anyone viewing their joint appearances on television. To voters still remembering Bush's incompetence and Cheney's intransigence, that incompatibility signaled a continued inability to govern. Some Republicans thought that the Democrats could run against Bush and Cheney for decades.

Even so, other election experts suggested later that the decisive moment in the 2012 election might have taken place during the primaries. When Caruso's nomination was still in doubt, a nationwide organization of retailers calling itself America's Storekeepers announced its support for Caruso, lauding his concern for below median income Americans.

The organization claimed to represent the country's low and midprice retailers, from the national "big box" chains to local mom-and-pop stores. Its rationale was no secret; the retailers were hurting and needed a candidate whose economic policies would help restore their profitability. Their personal loyalties to the Republican party notwithstanding, their responsibility to their companies and their shareholders required them to support Caruso.

Caruso himself was not overjoyed by the Storekeepers' endorsement. He enjoyed shopping once in a while but was uncomfortable with shopping as a significant mechanism for economic growth. The endorsement also lost Caruso some support among liberals, but the split in the business community created a political tsunami in the Republican party, and some commentators predicted that it would hurt the Republicans for a long time.

The commentators were right, for a decade later, a surprising proportion of corporate leaders supported the Democrats' progressive tax reforms. Even if they had to pay higher taxes, their companies would benefit from the resulting governmental spending.

CHAPTER TWO

HEALING THE ECONOMY

Caruso used his inaugural address to tell the country what, with the help of the Congress, he planned to do to heal the economy. His program would begin with some instant fixes to jump-start new economic activity, but he would then propose new job creation programs. These, he hoped, would compensate for the loss of jobs to the by now usual suspects: computerization and outsourcing, as well as the productivity increases that his grandfather had long ago excoriated as management speedups. He would also call for a program of long-range job creation that might not pay off until the 2020s or later, but that would, if all went well, not only create secure jobs but help reduce global warming and improve public education and health care.

Caruso pointed out that his job programs would raise productivity but until someone invented the free lunch, the economic changes would have to be paid for. Caruso hoped that the Pentagon's war budget could be reduced, but eventual tax reform was essential. He offered no details; too premature, he indicated, but he made clear that there would be no further tax reductions for the rich. And no one could predict what other economic reforms would be necessary in a world in which more countries were turning into economic superpowers and multinational corporations were expanding into multicontinentals.

INSTANT INCOME FIXES

A week later, Caruso announced his first income fix; he would ask Congress to send a one-time $2,000 of "jump-start money" to every family in the lowest quarter of the previous year's income distribution. It was an old idea and an expensive one, but targeting it to the least well off also signaled the start of a new, more egalitarian era, as well as an economic spur that would also please his business community allies. The Democratic party was happy too; grateful recipients might develop more party loyalty.

Caruso was hoping, with crossed fingers, that Congress would honor the traditional new president's honeymoon privileges, but some vocal members of the House were opposed to rewarding impecunious people who had probably neither worked nor voted—and some who were not even citizens. Ultimately Congress reduced the grant to $750 and limited it to citizens. It cut in the middle classes by allowing them to choose between a $750 tax exemption or a double tax deduction for the first $750 of their charitable contributions.

The jump-start set off the expected, if modest, buying splurge as poor and moderate income people replaced old clothes, computers, or furniture or made repairs to cars and houses. The splurge and the added middle class spending made small waves in other parts of the economy and created some jobs, and the Storekeepers were sure they had made the right political choice in backing Caruso.

Caruso's second instant income fix, although also a venerable idea, extended unemployment insurance for a further year, which Congress approved. However, Congress rejected his plan to provide at least three months of jobless insurance to all workers not now eligible for the program who could prove that they had been laid off recently.

Immediately afterward, centrist Democratic party leaders called on the president to stop doling out federal money. However, Caruso pointed out that the current deficit had been created almost entirely by the Republicans and the Democrats were not required to clean up their messes. Moreover, the Republican deficit had been incurred for fighting unnecessary wars and further enriching the very rich, while his additions to the deficit would pay for growing the economy.

Nonetheless, Caruso promised he would seek no further income supplements. Instead, a year later, he asked the Congress to raise the minimum wage annually until it was equivalent to the living wage, then already on the books in many communities. He also urged that the living wage be indexed to the average family income so that it would rise during good economic times when other incomes were rising.

The outcome, Caruso announced, would enable the United States to join other modern countries who had been traveling this path for much of the last century. The White House political team told the president not to hold his breath, for while the Congress agreed with Caruso in principle, it voted for only a year's increase in the minimum wage and limited it to adult earners working at least twenty hours a week.

The usual opposition from small businesses was complemented by resistance from industries facing competition from foreign low wage workers. In addition, Congress was fearful of possible effects on immigration. Some economists predicted that businesses that were unable or unwilling to pay higher wages would hire immigrants instead, which would surely result in additional Mexicans and other Latinos seeking to cross the border into the United States.

In 2016, the Caruso administration asked Congress once more to bring the minimum wage closer to the living wage, but again, the Congress voted only a single year's increase. Indeed, Caruso's dream of making the minimum wage equal to the living wage had to wait until 2026, Gordon's second year in the White House. Even then, some low wage labor jobs were excluded and continue to be so today. Hernandez hopes to end these exclusions soon so that by 2036 every worker will earn the living wage.

CREATING JOBS

As Caruso's support for income supplements and wage increases waned, he started talking up his job creation and preservation proposals. Seeking to disarm the likely opposition before the president submitted legislation, the White House hinted that, if necessary, it was ready to get into bed with private enterprise, especially if there was room for unions too.

Jennifer Grant, who occasionally doubled as the White House's informal ambassador to the business community, favored cost-plus contracts with private firms, with the government setting the profit rate as well as strict regulatory provisions that governed the contract. During one of the Caruso-Grant talks, the vice president reminded the audience of the deregulatory horrors of the past, which among other things later led to a small but potent citizens' lobby that testified or demonstrated against nearly every corporate or congressional deregulation scheme.

Grant also suggested that the Pentagon be brought into the job creation program. It always found money to spend on job-related R&D—and secretly enough to pursue risky schemes without political ill effects. By then, the Pentagon was eager to help; more men and women might enlist if they could work on peaceful projects. Grant and Caruso were delighted, for someday the Pentagon might be ready to turn down unnecessary military investments.

The White House initiative began in late 2013, but Caruso warned that quick job creation fixes were hard to find. However, he then immediately proposed such a fix. Announcing a national job search, he asked everyone—workers, executives, inventors, even schoolchildren—to report unfilled public and private needs in their areas that could be filled in labor-intensive ways.

The search was largely symbolic but also was intended to tell the public that government would henceforth regularly request its help. Later, Caruso asked elected officials to submit up to three old and new earmarks—also known as pork barrel projects—that, almost always being labor intensive, would help guarantee the early creation of jobs. The public was called on to help weed out useless projects and suggest better ones, although the Government Accountability Office eventually did most of the weeding.

Given their bad reputation, the resort to earmarks was politically risky, but the Caruso administration persuaded the many congressional supporters of the venture to set up stringent cost effectiveness tests. For example, earmark applicants had to determine the number of jobs and permanent jobs likely to be created directly or indirectly per million dollars of federal money invested. Applicants who guaranteed to hire the largest number of jobless adults were ranked more highly than the rest.

The tests and measures never worked quite as well as they did on paper, but their mere existence set standards that helped eliminate the worst earmarks and, twenty years later, have transformed them into a respectable form of public investment.

The Republican administration that took office in 2020 ended Grant's cost-plus scheme and gave private firms more control over costs, profits, and regulation. However, with money tight and old formulas for demonizing government no longer as credible as in the past, the Republican reprivatization was not successful. When Gordon became president in 2024, she asked the Congress to let the Departments of Labor and Commerce to work together to establish labor-intensive public businesses that private enterprise would not touch.

Gordon's bill was drafted so loosely that under certain conditions, government agencies could even compete with private firms. Although all of the business lobbies and organizations, including former Storekeepers attacked the bill, politicians liked the patronage possibilities, and eventually, the federal government manufactured reasonably priced auto parts, low cost furniture, and healthy cereals for young children. Hernandez has already promised that he will try to have the government market new drugs that resulted from government research.

Needless to say, the business community also challenged the bill in the courts. By now, two decades had passed since the Bush administration left the White House and Caruso and Gordon had appointed enough liberal justices to reform the federal bench. In 2031, the bill survived its final test in the Supreme Court, and the principle that under certain conditions, government could compete with private enterprise was established.

Slowing Outsourcing's Job Drain

When Caruso first arrived in the Oval Office, he was under immediate pressure to do something about the steady job drain from outsourcing. However, what began as an instant job fix has, like other government projects, taken many years.

The drain in unskilled jobs has so far been the easiest to reduce. As wages rose overseas, including in the third world, and higher oil prices drove up the cost of shipping, a number of goods requiring mostly low or semiskilled labor can now be produced here. Even services are affected: overseas back offices are now really cheap only in countries in which few people speak English.

Outsourcing of footloose high skill jobs has been more difficult to slow down. The government has tried to replace the departed skilled jobs by encouraging inventions and innovations that give America a temporary leg up in the international competition. Admittedly, the task is Sisyphean: new goods and services have to be invented all the time because the jobs created by earlier inventions often migrate overseas.

Consequently, the Hernandez administration has now asked Congress to prevent outsourcing by firms whose products or services were initially created by government research grants. It is also ready to offer financial support to firms that agree to put off outsourcing for at least ten to twenty years. Hernandez is confident that political support from unions and worker lobbies will be sufficient to counter the opposition from the business community. And by midcentury, twenty years hence, international wage equalization trends could make outsourcing virtually obsolete.

LONG-RANGE JOB CREATION

From the start, the Caruso administration's preferred way of growing a healthy economy was long-term job creation. Soon after the inauguration, the White House put its newly created Council of Long-Range Advisers to work to screen suggestions from citizens and public officials for the types of jobs that would result in the economically and socially most productive long-term payoffs. The Council proposed job programs in what is now called the global warming industry and public education, topping them off with an innovative and labor-intensive health care scheme.

Fighting Global Warming

Global warming had become such a hot topic in the first decade of the century that the Congress voted at once and almost unanimously for jobs that would speed up attempts to reduce the various kinds of global warming. Experts on the politics of global warming realized that new jobs might divert attention from the political and other difficulties of achieving really significant reductions in carbon dioxide emissions, but elected officials were glad that for a little while longer they could postpone making voters give up their SUVs.

The first job programs speeded up the production of solar panels as well as the development of wind farms. Subsidizing builders to include solar panels on all new construction and rehabilitation projects not only added jobs in the factories producing them but reduced their price. As a result, owners of individual homes and multifamily housing in sunny climates could be tempted with tax reductions to replace all or parts of their roofs.

Wind farm development followed the same strategy although not in my backyard (NIMBY) movements kept the farms away from residential, recreational, and agricultural areas. At one point, the White House even proposed renting land in Canada's frozen northern region; after that, it urged the United Nations to develop a worldwide development plan. The most ingenious scheme, which has not yet gotten off the ground, is to locate the windmills in newly planted forests that will eventually hide the wind farms but never grow tall enough to interfere with the operation of the windmills.

Job creation money is now hastening the construction of higher density housing and the expansion of mass transit, as well as a nationwide reforesting program, especially near industrial areas that spew the largest amounts of carbon dioxide into the atmosphere. The same jobs program is paying for the construction of experimental seawalls in low lying and hurricane-prone coastal areas so that the country will be ready if and when serious flooding begins. Some of the experimental seawalls will be factory produced modules.

Although the United Nations is still working on dividing up the responsibilities and opportunities related to the melting of the glaciers and the permafrost in the Arctic and Antarctic regions, American workers will receive a share of the work. Oil, metal, and shipping route explorations will begin soon, and there are even jobs for biologists, breeders, and others seeking to grow polar bears, penguins, and less picturesque fauna and flora that can adapt to the planet's formerly frozen regions.

The Small Class Initiative

Soon after Hernandez became Caruso's point man in the Department of Education, it inaugurated the Small Class Initiative, federalizing earlier state and local efforts to reduce class size in the nation's public schools. Based on the many research findings about the positive educational effects of small classes, the Initiative provided funding for school districts prepared to establish or add small classes eventually to consist of no more than fifteen students. Although the Initiative began slowly, over the years, it has created many teaching jobs as well as construction work to build new classrooms.

The scarcity of money, teachers, and classrooms to meet the demand required that the program be incremental. Young parents and their lobbies wanted to begin with classes for preschoolers, which would concurrently alleviate their day care problems. Public and nonprofit antipoverty agencies urged starting with preschool classes reserved for poor communities, giving their children the informal education that middle and upper class children normally received at home. Affluent school districts argued that they deserved first priority because they were training an inordinate share of the nation's future leaders, although in fact few were eligible because their classes were already small.

Congress ended the impasse by starting with kindergarten classes as well as with high school classes in districts suffering from the highest drop out rates and largest classes. Over the years, Congress increased the program when the funds, classrooms, and trained teachers were available and slowed it down when federal funds were scarce or the deficits reached politically dangerous levels. At such times, the program was placed on a cost sharing basis with local school districts.

The program was slowed by other problems. An inadequate supply of teachers prepared for small class instruction had to be corrected. Local school boards that opposed federal interference in school affairs had to be pacified with federal promises not to interfere in curricular matters or to do so only with federal funds. The subsidized education ventures are described in chapter 6, "Schoolings."

In her last State of the Union speech in 2032, Gordon could announce that over the years, the Initiative had created almost a million additional teaching jobs. Some of the new teachers had been recruited from dying sectors of the economy, and now that small classes have made teaching easier and more stimulating, even graduates of selective colleges are seeking careers in public education.

The Day Care Initiative

The impetus for the Day Care Initiative came from breadwinner families with young children who charged that the Small Class Initiative ignored their needs. Accordingly, Hernandez in his capacity as Secretary of Education established a pilot program in which the federal government paid for a share of the new day care, nursery school, and pre-kindergarten programs. The day care workers would receive some teacher training so as to beef up the educational component of day care and so that they would be able to fill in when they were needed by the small classes program.

The professional day care establishment was not pleased with the new competition, nor were poor people who provided paid day care at home for relatives, friends, and neighbors. The federal government would have preferred to let local communities settle the conflicts, except that parallel battles, spurred by, among others, the professional day care lobbies, erupted in participating federal agencies.

The turf battles took years to resolve, but eventually, the day care establishment received some supervisory responsibility for in-school day care. When the federal budget is flush, school-based day care staffs supply some educational input to the remaining out-of-school day care facilities as well as to in-home day care providers who request it.

Debates over possible deleterious developmental effects of day care have never ended, and advocates of traditional "family values" have demanded federal financial assistance for stay at home parenting. They may get their wish, for not long after he arrived in the Oval Office, Hernandez asked the Congress to subsidize jobless parents, as well as involuntary part-time workers, who stay home to take care of their children. If the Congress agrees, the government will finally recognize officially that child rearing ought to be paid work.

INVENTING THE NURSE-DOCTOR

The Caruso administration's most dramatic job creation initiative was the invention of the so-called nurse-doctor, or N-D. N-Ds are trained nurses and nurse practitioners who also receive basic general medical training. Thus, they can provide the routine medical care that in the past had traditionally taken up most of the time and energy of the MDs, whether they were caring for children's respiratory infections or monitoring the chronic illnesses of the older patients they saw regularly. MDs are now able to devote more time to complicated cases, including those referred to them by the N-Ds. Specialists can concentrate on the care for which they have been trained.

Legend has it that the N-D program was hatched at a White House brainstorming session when a young staffer asked about the Chinese barefoot doctors said to have been the early mainstay of the Communist health care system. Actually, the N-D was derived from the practice, begun earlier in the century, of nursing schools offering doctorates in nursing in an effort to increase nurses' training and raise their professional status.

Then several state health departments suggested offering medical training for some of these nurses for parts of the country short of doctors. After a year of battles with national and other medical associations who opposed the program, a handful of nursing and medical schools undertook a pilot program to train nurses as doctors. A year later, the Secretary of the newly established U.S. Department of Public Health enlarged the pilot program, and by the end of Caruso's first term, she testified to Congress that the first N-Ds provided not only additional but also improved medical care.

The Secretary of Public Health also persuaded Caruso to include

N-Ds in his long-range job creation program. Caruso needed little persuading since the program has been very popular from the start, and the voters—as well as patients' lobbies—have demanded its expansion even when federal funds were scarce. Evaluation studies have found that many patients are improving faster than before, especially when N-Ds are given sufficient time to listen to patients and supply "tender loving care." Patients reported being more comfortable talking to the N-Ds than to the MDs, who, because they are higher in status, can be intimidating even when they try hard not to be. Moreover, MDs are still being trained to heal diseases and bodies while nurses have always been expected to treat people.

Now that the program is in full swing, it is also creating jobs in significant numbers. But not everyone has been happy. The HMOs and insurance companies have long been worried about what might happen if the N-Ds become too popular and start to replace doctors. As more N-Ds appear on the scene, MDs are turning nervous too, and the organized medical profession fears that the N-Ds will be even more threatening to its control of medical care than the practitioners of alternative medicine.

Moreover, turf battles erupted early on, particularly when N-Ds decided that they knew the patients better than the supervising MDs and were therefore entitled to play a bigger role in the referral process. In some places they have done so; in many others, the MDs held on, using their credentials to put the N-Ds in their place. Even nurses have gotten into the fight, for the N-Ds are just as protective of their position as MDs and, standing between the MDs and the nurses, they have further reduced the status of the latter in the medical pecking order.

Medicare and Supercare

The nurse-doctors made another, totally unexpected contribution to the country's well-being. Because most are on salary and even those in private practice charge less than MDs, they reduced the overall cost of that care sufficiently to join a final political push that would bring full single payer medical care to America.

However, many in the business community pushed too, notably the firms and industries competing with foreign countries supplying publicly financed health care. They had been pressing the federal government to take over health care for several years, although other parts of the business community wanted to maintain health care and health insurance as profit-seeking institutions.

In 2018, with one eye on the 2020 election, the supporters of various single payer systems met with the candidates from both parties. Caruso, seeking to help his vice president move into the Oval Office, jumped the gun and asked Congress to turn Medicare into a universal program that would eventually also incorporate Medicaid and the Veterans Administration.

The medical, hospital, and health insurance organizations and their lobbies as well as the remaining fighters in the conservative ideological phalanx immediately revived their array of past attacks on "socialized medicine," "medical bureaucracy," and other traditional demons. Still, even the ideologues had to admit that American capitalism could not compete in the global economy without government help. Caruso, knowing that a universal Medicare had widespread and strong support, invited all the involved parties to a meeting at Camp David.

Shortly afterward, Caruso reported to the nation the agreement that they had reached. Congress willing, the scope of the Medicare program would be extended over the next several years, but employers would pay a medical tax during those years to compensate the taxpayers for taking over the payment of workers' health insurance. In addition, employers would act in various ways to reduce the need for avoidable medical care. For example, they agreed to improve workplace safety programs and to support legislation to strengthen the Occupational Safety and Health Act, Workers Compensation, and other federal worker safety programs. They also promised to support the inclusion of the N-Ds in the Medicare program and to back the N-Ds' proposal to offer preventative care.

Another part of the Camp David deal led to the creation of Supercare, a partially subsidized fee-for-service system that would provide higher status medical care, and pacify the HMOs and insurance companies. It now serves people able and willing to pay MDs and even specialists to be their general physicians, offers faster elective surgery, and offers patients a role in selecting their prescription medicines.

The HMOs and other insurers were brought on board in other ways, including a new medical malpractice insurance program for MDs and N-Ds, as well as an expanded federally aided long-term-care insurance program for old people eager to live out their lives at home. In addition, Caruso agreed to help the health insurers and the private hospitals to establish and fund luxury hospitals that would serve the rich exclusively, as well as recovery resorts for them.

Liberal and radicals were appalled by the establishment of a two-price medical care system, and their representatives in Congress voted against subsidizing Supercare. Privately, Caruso wished he could vote with the liberals, but publicly, he insisted that such systems existed in other countries operating under the single payer system. Establishing Supercare would also keep both systems on their medical toes. Later, the liberals realized that without Supercare and the luxury recovery resorts, Caruso could not have obtained the needed support for his medical reforms.

Although what is now known as the second Camp David agreement required only four weekends (in addition to an uncounted number of person-hours of staff time among the participants), Congress took more than a year to approve the final package. Implementing and fine-tuning the new system have taken several more years, especially because the O'Hara administration tried unsuccessfully to reprivatize Medicare, increase the subsidy for Supercare, and cut back on the N-D program.

Gordon ran for the presidency promising to take down the roadblocks the O'Hara administration set up for Medicare, and toward the end of her first term, the Gordon administration began to reduce government funding for Supercare. Hernandez has suggested that he will try to privatize it completely by 2034.

The Gordon administration sometimes used Supercare as a role model for improving Medicare, for example, by creating public recovery hotels. And now Hernandez has promised that N-Ds will be making emergency house calls as soon as the needed funds are available.

THE BEGINNINGS OF TAX REFORM

When Caruso began to revive a stagnant wage economy, the Republicans immediately attacked him both as a free-spending liberal and as a Bush-imitating deficit enlarger. Thus, he took care early on to say repeatedly that once the economy was stronger, tax increases would be necessary. The Caruso-Grant show even spent a couple of installments describing the pros and cons of existing and new taxes that could help the government pay its bills.

After the 2014 midterm election, Caruso bit the tax bullet, but he did so slowly and very carefully. Taking what he sometimes called the economic justice route, he asked for more power to collect the hundreds of billions of evaded and unpaid taxes still owed the government. He persuaded Congress to beef up the relevant Internal Revenue Service bureaus and in a daring political move had them pay special attention to large campaign contributors, the thousand richest Americans, and the firms that had benefited most lavishly from Bush's endless outsourcing of government functions and funds to the Republicans' allies in the corporate world.

Looking for other taxes that would only impact a small number of people and firms, Caruso then asked for an increase in the estate tax. In addition, however, he proposed an Earned Estate Tax Credit that would enable all Americans to end their lives with an estate and to pass on money or property or both to their children. The estate tax credit idea was actually Gordon's, but Caruso did not properly credit her invention until he campaigned for her in the 2024 election.

The Congress was not eager to increase the estate tax but was so enthusiastic about the Earned Estate Tax Credit that a majority of the House and Senate called for passing it immediately. In one of his informal talks from which Grant was excused, Caruso responded regretfully that the economy—and the government's tax receipts— would have to grow first and asked Congress also to approve the increase in the estate tax.

For the rest of that year, estate tax reform legislation was debated and amended, but when it was finally approved, Caruso's supporters were sure that his universal estate proposal had made the difference. The 2016 Earned Estate Tax Credit bill guaranteed that parents without funds or property would be able to pass a $10,000 estate to every descendant whom they had raised as a child for at least ten years.

Although the amount was nominal and the Treasury Department was not sure how the tax credit would be financed, the idea that everyone should be able to leave something to the next generation was immensely popular. Every campaigning presidential candidate since has expressed the hope that the amount can soon be raised.

The Landslide Tax Bill

Caruso's landslide victory in the 2016 election emboldened him to suggest that the deficit could not be raised further and that new taxes had to be found. The only question was which taxes. With the baby boomers' retirement about to peak, he insisted on turning FICA into a progressive tax and removing its cap. He also asked Congress for a personal income tax hike on the largest incomes, but except for some loophole closings, he kept business taxes at nearly their present level so as not to inhibit the willingness of private enterprise to preserve and grow jobs. Still, Caruso could not resist trying something new, and he added a national consumption tax on luxuries to the tax package.

Caruso had always thought that everyone ought to be allowed and even encouraged to make as much money as they could, playing all the income maximizing games of their choice, as long as they hurt no one and paid out the public's share at tax time. He also believed that those who successfully played the biggest games should pay a greater share, and therefore he wanted a more steeply progressive income tax for the country's very highest individual and corporate earners.

Consequently, Caruso asked Congress for a maximum tax rate of 60 percent once total annual income exceeded five times the national median family income (almost $55,000 in 2016) and a 75 percent maximum when total annual income exceeded ten times the median, with some variations for large cost of living differences around the country. Tying the tax to median income would allow the government to benefit when the median income rose and share the pain when it fell.

The anti-tax lobbies resorted to old arguments that the high income earners were already paying the largest share of the total collected income tax. This time, however, the administration chose to counter the old arguments, first by reporting the number of big businesses and highly paid individuals who still owed money to the federal government and the total amount they owed in uncollected taxes. At the same time, bloggers circulated the names alleged to be at the top of the Internal Revenue Service list, several of whom were also leaders of anti-tax lobbies.

Then Caruso established the Tax Avoidance Division in the Internal Revenue Service and a companion one in the Department of Justice to go after the deadbeats. Congress got the point and, although the vote was very close, added a law to eliminate the most egregious loopholes in business taxes. After some downward reductions in Caruso's numbers, Congress approved the income tax hike as well.

The corporate lobbyists and their friends in the Congress were so pleased with Caruso's decision not to raise corporate taxes at this time that they did not contest the loophole legislation. They could not have opposed it publicly anyway, and besides, even Caruso could not foresee the loopholes they would lobby for in future tax laws.

The consumption tax did not survive, however. The conservative punditry claimed that this tax would end the way of life Americans had endorsed by putting conservatives in the White House for most of the last several decades. The yacht builders reminded the country of how badly their industry had been damaged by an earlier such tax, but Caruso's base rebelled too. People for whom luxuries were a rarely affordable treat did not want to pay additional taxes when a windfall or a lucky bet allowed them to treat themselves.

The Obscene Profits Tax

After the 2018 midterms, Caruso was a lame duck but decided he would put two more tax ideas on the table. One was a new approach to business taxation that he thought would keep most of his business community friends on his side: an obscene or exorbitant profits tax that, in effect, asked the country to draw a line between acceptable and unacceptable profits.

The firms that earned excessive profits expressed their opposition to their friends in high political places. As the 2020 election loomed, they came out for Frank O'Hara after it became apparent that, among the Republican candidates, he had launched the harshest attacks on the idea that profits could be obscene. Conservative ideologues chimed in as well, agreeing to a person that capitalism could not survive a cap on profits. The religious Right noted that calling profits obscene reflected the economic debauchery of the atheist Left.

Caruso was not surprised by the response, but he asked the National Science Foundation to launch a grant program that would give the notion of obscene profit scientific legitimacy. Research reports and scholarly articles were written, and very slowly and gingerly, mainstream economists began to consider whether profits could be obscene or at least exorbitant. After all, some had always treated windfall profits ambivalently.

After the Republican victory in 2020, O'Hara terminated all federal support for the research on profit. Others, including the Democracy Project, took up the slack, and in 2025, barely a year after Gordon sat down in the Oval Office, she brought up the obscene profits tax once more.

This time, the public attacks turned out to be relatively mild, for neither the corporations nor the very wealthy owners of family firms could easily defend obscene profits. Arguments that maximum profit was the cornerstone of capitalism failed to carry much weight in an era of ever larger multinational corporations. True, hedge funds, some academic endowment funds, and other institutions concentrating on high risk investments still objected strongly, and the credit card industry was described as going "bonkers."

The Treasury Department quietly added a moratorium for infant industries and a short-term loophole for the high risk financial market. As a result, the people who spoke for the business community decided that as long as they could try to make a little more money than everyone else, they could live with an exorbitant profits tax. It would hurt only the rotten apples who gave capitalism a bad name.

Consequently, Gordon decided to come up with a tough tax proposal: all firms earning double their industry's median profit, as a proportion of gross income, over a five-year period would be taxed half the excess profit. She knew Congress would never go that far, and so she added various reductions for good behavior, for example, for firms creating new jobs with their extra profits.

Even so, Congress finally said no, and later investigative reporters discovered that developers and entertainment executives who made lavish contributions to national election campaigns had convinced enough Democrats to vote in favor of a seemingly innocuous motion that actually sank the bill. Subsequently, the Treasury Department figured out that the same tax receipts could be obtained by a more progressive tax on business income, and such a tax eventually made it through the Congress.

Still, the national debate over an obscene profits tax paid off. Moral questions about profit and pricing habits were put on the public agenda, and business journalists now reported regularly and in more detail when companies announced very high profits. As a result, firms and whole industries depending on the goodwill of their customers persuaded their shareholders to go for reduced prices that might increase business further instead of being tarred with economic obscenity.

Moreover, Gordon would occasionally issue sound bites still favoring an obscene profits tax, and Hernandez has already indicated that he will reintroduce it if the right political climate develops during economic emergencies. He would, however, levy it only on firms engaged in speculation and those supplying goods and services that could be defined as necessities.

THE WEALTH TAX

Caruso's second lame duck tax idea was a wealth tax that would levy an annual 1/2 percent tax on the wealth of the richest 1 percent of Americans. Jennifer Grant had objected strongly to his introducing it, arguing that even mentioning another new tax would seriously damage her chances of winning the 2020 presidential election. As a result, the Treasury Department was asked to compare the virtues of a higher income tax—as much as 90 percent of the last $5 million in income—to those of a wealth tax. The study was never completed, for Caruso was sure that as global economic forces continued to weaken the domestic economy, the government would have to play an ever greater role in that economy whether it wanted to or not. Consequently, he believed a wealth tax was inevitable, and he thought he might as well reserve his place in history for having suggested it.

Needless to say, the mere mention of even a nominal wealth tax created a record flood of opinions, most from very wealthy people or their spokespersons. Almost all insisted that Americans were entitled to hold onto whatever wealth they could acquire and save, and some neoconservative intellectuals insisted that the entitlement constituted the essence of American exceptionalism.

In the past, a large number of nonaffluent Americans had regularly told the pollsters they still had a chance to become rich. However, polls conducted after Caruso came out for the wealth tax found that many low, moderate, and even middle income people now seemed to realize that neither they nor their children would ever become rich. Under certain conditions, a majority might possibly even support a wealth tax.

The government's tax experts went to work to show that the wealth tax would not have adverse effects on needed private investment and on the overall health of the economy. Wall Street liberals who supported Caruso proposed giving the Federal Reserve Bank the right to adjust the wealth tax annually: down if it wanted to encourage investment, up if the federal budget needed replenishing.

Caruso had only raised a trial balloon, knowing that it might have to be raised a few more times before there was a chance it would fly. His balloon came down quickly, for the threatened arrival of another minirecession gave congressional conservatives and centrists a reason to bury the idea in several study committees.

Undaunted, Caruso launched another balloon: the wealth tax would be levied only on those who had earned their riches with government funds or through government-funded or government-supported inventions and other activities. In fact, he pointed out, the very rich would not even be taxed for their wealth but merely be asked to return part of the money they made with government help. According to the pollsters, the general public liked the idea better than Caruso's earlier wealth tax, and so did the self-made, the people who could fairly claim that they were entitled to all the fruits of their own labor.

The limited support for the bill by the well off shrank dramatically once they discovered how much they were indebted to the government. The list included not only those who had grown rich from the profits of all military contractors and weapons makers, most medical and pharmaceutical firms, and large portions of industrial agriculture but anyone who had invested in the cyberspace and related industries that lived off the government's initial development of the Internet. Even the rich descendants of slave traders were on the list.

In fact almost every very wealthy person was indebted somehow to the government, which gave the tax writing congressional committees an excuse to table the bill. Most Republicans and even some Democrats did not want to know how much the laissez-faire capitalism they worshipped rested on public monies.

The Return of the Wealth Tax

When Grant lost the 2020 presidential election to O'Hara by a close margin, she blamed her loss on Caruso's eagerness to introduce the wealth tax. Eighteen months later, Grant had to apologize to Caruso, for to everyone's surprise including his own, O'Hara announced that he would have to ask Congress to pass a wealth tax. It would be a midget compared to Caruso's proposal, he assured his supporters, but he really had no choice.

O'Hara had won the 2020 election in part because of the onset of the recession. However, the newest downturn reduced the government's income even as the costs of Caruso's job creation programs were still rising. Fighting global warming, building the new classrooms, and hiring the new teachers for the small classes program were expensive, and getting the N-D health program under way was becoming even more so. In addition, O'Hara had promised to reduce the deficit and needed higher tax receipts.

O'Hara slowed down school building and N-D recruitment and made a number of other budget cuts that followed the standard Republican playbook. However, most of Caruso's innovations were too popular to be terminated completely. Also, Caruso had just raised the income tax, and O'Hara could not increase the corporate income tax further until Medicare was paying most of the bills for worker health care.

The time had therefore come, O'Hara announced, for the very wealthy to pay a greater share of the country's bills, especially those who had enjoyed enormous wealth for generations. Since so few paid an estate tax, he would now have to propose a minimal wealth tax: 1/10 percent of all wealth over $10 million, not counting housing and other basic assets.

Even though O'Hara was a loyal Republican, the last part of his argument contained some personal input. O'Hara was rich, but he was also a self-made man who had been humiliated more than once too often by the old wealth crowd during his many years as a Republican party fund-raiser.

Despite the modesty of O'Hara's proposal, old wealth and new lined up quickly in opposition to his proposal. However, many people who usually insisted that government had no right to tax their yet nonexistent wealth now supported O'Hara. Although some conservatives talked of impeaching O'Hara, the Republican party leadership, in the Congress and elsewhere, was stuck. The party had to support its president, and since most Democrats were also in favor of the tax, it passed by a higher than expected margin.

Meanwhile, court challenges to the tax filed during the Caruso presidency had wound their way up the federal courts and reached the Supreme Court. To the surprise of many, a 6–3 majority ruled that the tax was constitutional, which was also the strongest of a series of signals that the conservative hold over the Supreme Court was ending.

Nonetheless, the O'Hara wealth tax was so minute and full of loopholes that less than ten thousand taxpayers had to pay it during O'Hara's years in office. As a result, the expected capital flight did not materialize, but the economy did not flourish, and the deficit continued to grow. In November 2024, the Republican interregnum was over.

Gordon and the Wealth Tax

Foreign observers who visited the United States during the 2024 primary and election campaigns were amazed how little the leading candidates said either about the continued disconnect between the profit economy and the wage and salary economy or about taxes. Still, all the presidential candidates knew that whoever won the election would have to call for more taxes, and soon after Gordon had settled into the Oval Office, the Treasury Department set up an informal task force to reinstate the process begun during the Caruso years.

Nominally, the task force was supposed to discuss taxation in general and particularly what taxes lent themselves to an increase. However, word came down from the White House that Gordon wanted to resuscitate Caruso's version of the wealth tax. Gordon had already brought up the wealth tax in her campaign not only as a moneymaker for the government but as a building block for a fairer America and a healthier democracy. Caruso's economic policies had sought to improve the economic position of the below median income population, but now the time had come to reduce the gap between the richest Americans and the rest of America another way.

The task force decided its task was to persuade the wealthy to accept the wealth tax. An economic sociologist in the group told her colleagues about the connection between the acquisition of wealth and the acquisition of status. Beyond a certain level of wealth, what mattered most was *socially marginal* wealth, having just somewhat more than the peers and competitors with whom the rich, like everyone else, compared themselves.

Instead of amassing the largest amount of money and other riches, perhaps the wealthiest individuals and families could be convinced to strive just to be a little richer than the richest Joneses and, of course, to be rewarded for it socially. Whether the Joneses were worth $100 million or $150 million did not matter; the name of the game was to outpace them. Furthermore, if competing at the lower level could be seen as a patriotic act, then someday the very wealthy might even compete to pay the highest wealth tax. Moreover, the competition over a marginal advantage did not even have to be restricted to wealth. Perhaps honors and other symbolic awards could play a supplementary role as well.

Backed up by data from a team of economists and investigative reporters about how much the very wealthy actually spent, the task force also argued that the richest Americans lacked the time and energy to spend all the money they amassed. True, they could invest the rest, but since they could not spend the resulting profits, a higher wealth tax might not feel as painful as they imagined.

Some optimists even claimed that once the very wealthy could be persuaded to pursue a relative advantage rather than an absolute one, corporate executives might be less inclined to insist on enormous pay packages and investors might have less reason to speculate. With fewer speculators in the wings, Wall Street might even reduce its pressure for maximal short-run profits, thereby encouraging firms to pursue long-term growth.

Ultimately, the task force concluded that years of debate and experience would have to pass before the very wealthy would look at great wealth from this angle. Perhaps the persuasive process would not hit pay dirt until a new generation had become used to the wealth tax.

In 2026, just after the midterm elections, Gordon introduced legislation for her wealth tax. Building on O'Hara's start, the bill called for a 1 percent tax on all wealth over $3 million, sheltered or not, rising gradually until it reached 10 percent of all wealth over $500 million and 15 percent of all wealth over $1 billion.

The task force had urged Gordon to start high because they were sure that after the wealthy had their say, Congress would reduce the amount and add loopholes, most of which might not be closed for years to come. Of course they were right, and the Congress soon halved the Gordon percentages. It also killed a section that proposed an additional tax for all wealth created by speculation, at that time particularly by hedge fund managers.

Before that, and to no one's surprise, the opposition to the wealth tax pulled out all the stops in its campaign to sink the tax. The campaign organizers were consummate professionals; they made sure that those speaking for them were themselves not wealthy. Instead, they sent the beneficiaries of untaxed wealth: high officials and some very poor clients of major charities; also presidents of and scholarship students from selective colleges, and famous actors from nonprofit theater groups, among others, all of them testifying how irreparably the wealth tax would damage their institutions.

Other speakers, many of them local business leaders working for Wall Street lobbyists, traveled all over the country announcing that the very wealthy people who indirectly provided communities with jobs would move their factories or offices elsewhere if local politicians would not fight the wealth tax. Mayors of suburbs, weekend communities, and vacation or skiing resorts where the very rich gathered were lobbied as well.

The Gordon administration fought back, mobilizing its liberal, union, and citizen lobby supporters as if they were preparing for a presidential election. A special effort sent people into below median income areas asking residents to send personal messages to their representatives.

In addition, Gordon's task force showed people how few ordinary Americans had ever struck it rich over the years. The group inspired studies of conspicuous consumption and made sure that these included dramatic examples of outrageous spending.

A group of American historians issued a study that reported how the best known of the wealthiest individuals and families had obtained their money, and for good measure the study indicated how much of the country's old wealth came from slave trading, piracy, and other morally dubious ventures. Rubbing in the message a bit further, the Internal Revenue Service put together a list of the country's hundred wealthiest families and showed how little some had paid in total federal taxes over the last half century and how much they had spent on partying. Needless to say, the findings were leaked to several political Web sites the day after the list had been put together.

While the battle over the wealth tax was heating up, Gordon asked the Congress to enact a new national honors program, with medals being awarded to people who had contributed to the public interest in unusually great measure in a variety of fields and endeavors. Gordon wished she could just give medals to rich people who supported the wealth tax, with a special one to the plutocrat who would pay the highest wealth tax.

Everyone thought the wealth tax that Congress had already reduced in committee would pass with enough votes to spare, but at the last minute, Gordon had to twist a couple of arms so that the bill could survive a Senate filibuster. Washington should not have been surprised, but the very wealthy and the organizations they controlled or influenced could still get to elected officials in the old ways and with old forms of persuasion.

Before the tax passed, the very wealthiest Americans had begun to move capital out of the country. The Gordon administration quietly slipped a provision into the bill that initially taxed wealth held five years earlier rather than current wealth. That measure reduced the capital flight, and the Treasury Department decided that the remaining loss of capital was an unavoidable cost of the wealth tax.

By now, most countries had been taxing wealth for many years, and so with some exceptions, high returns from capital flight funds were possible only in some third world countries where investments also entailed considerable risk. Still, the White House let it be known that countries welcoming fleeing capital would be penalized with cuts in foreign aid.

White House lawyers, working together with citizen lobbies and other supporters of the wealth tax, spent much of Gordon's first term fighting legislative, legal, and administrative attempts to add loopholes that would nullify or sabotage the tax. However, by the middle of her second term, Gordon could report that the tax was beginning to be collected. Party researchers and citizen journalists in the blogging world even dug up several well known venture capitalists who testified that they were enjoying life more now that they could no longer consume as conspicuously as before.

THE FUTURE OF WORK

Gordon used her 2030 State of the Union address to celebrate the passage of the new wealth tax and to announce that her administration could now begin to put the programs created during the Caruso years and her first term (including some discussed in later chapters of this book) on a more solid financial footing.

Steve Hernandez, fearing that a tax backlash could damage his forthcoming campaign for the White House, pressed Gordon not to propose any new taxes, and Gordon promised him that she would avoid doing so. Hernandez later made the same promise in the 2032 election campaign and stressed that his running mate had once been a banker.

Gordon had already planned to devote her lame duck years to the future of work and the problems associated with it. Like Caruso, she had long believed that full-time work, especially decently paid work, was on a permanently downward trend. To be sure, the graphs still pictured a roller coaster and in good economic times, some economists thought the employment problem had been solved. But their thinking boomeranged in bad times, and every recovery peaked below the levels of the last one.

The story was trite now, but job-destroying forces were still sweeping through the economy and reinforcing the development of a four-level wage economy. Three of the levels were familiar: full-time workers holding thirty-five hour a week jobs; the involuntary part-timers, many working less than twenty hours; and the jobless. However, a fourth and rapidly growing level consisted of full-time employees putting in thirty hours a week or less because there was not enough work for them, sometimes even when the economy was on an upswing.

Meanwhile, the number of people who wanted or needed to work was going up. The first grandchildren of the initial post–World War II baby boomers were now entering the labor market. New immigrants were still arriving, and many, along with prior arrivals, were reproducing at an above average rate. In addition, more older people wanted or had to work past their sixty-fifth birthdays.

Poorly paid workers could be helped by reducing their FICA payments. Or Congress could once more raise the Earned Income Tax Credit payments, at least as long as the tax paying strata were able and willing to supply the funds—and other parts of the population were able and willing to hold their feet, and those of elected officials, to the political fire.

Inequality of work time was less easily reversed, but Gordon called in her Council of Economic Advisers. After their usual meetings with elected officials and the national appeal for ideas that Caruso had initiated about twenty years earlier, they came up with three proposals.

The first proposal called for work sharing, moving toward an across the board equalization of work hours. This equalization could be achieved by requiring an earlier onset of overtime pay: at thirty hours rather than the then current thirty-six hours. Nearly a century earlier, President Roosevelt had used the same concept to bring the workweek down from forty-eight hours.

The economic advisers were not sure, however, whether work sharing would achieve its aim. In theory, employers should hire more workers to avoid overtime pay, but in practice, they might instead shorten the workweek and demand more productivity from their workers, especially if wages were not to be reduced. Moreover, in workplaces in which expensive machinery was running 24/7, employers might resort to more automation or outsourcing.

The second proposal would encourage more people to leave the labor force. In addition to new incentives for late entry for young people and for earlier retirement by the middle aged and old, the Council proposed an annual stipend to those who volunteered to stay out of the labor force for a period of at least three to five years.

Critics questioned whether new incentives for the young and the old could be invented or whether enough people would be willing to give up work for several years. Those pursuing careers could not afford to drop out, but even those who held routine jobs would be fearful that the labor market might not take them back. Aspiring artists, writers, and performers could be expected to sign up, but the annual stipend might also attract people who simply did not want to work. Even amateur politicians could see angry taxpayers protesting that their taxes were supporting layabouts.

The third proposal, for the creation of a new government program, was intended for the people now working full-time but less than thirty hours as well as the involuntary part-timers. Basing the program's title on the twentieth-century notion of the government as employer of last resort, the Council of Economic Advisers called it the Community Service Work Program (CSWP). CSWP would provide eligible workers part-time employment in federal, state, and local public agencies at the living wage and bring their workweek back to 35 hours.

People working less than thirty hours a week in their main jobs could put in an extra five to seven hours a week—and involuntary part-time workers even more. In periods when enough federal money was available, extra work hours could be added and eligibility extended to the seventy- or eighty-year-olds who still wanted, or had, to work. The public agencies receiving workers could restore services eliminated during budget cutbacks, expand existing programs, and even add new ones that might be staffed by workers funded by CSWP.

Congress was tired and sent all three proposals into the further studies limbo, but Gordon appealed to the unions and employee lobbies to persuade their elected representatives. Soon afterward, the Congress approved a three-year test of CSWP in a handful of states and local communities ready to establish the new program.

The early results came in after Hernandez had been elected president, and they have been mainly positive. CSWP applicants who were given a choice of jobs usually chose local helping agencies over the rest, picked the easiest or more interesting kinds of work, and rarely volunteered to do the dirty work. Consequently, agencies needing people for a little extra dirty work would have to pay more than the living wage. In that case, Hernandez noted with pleasure, at least some people doing the dirtiest work might finally be paid the higher wages that they have always deserved.

Some CSWP workers have found their jobs so satisfying that they are applying for full-time jobs in the public agencies. Even most of those who put in only five to seven hours report a greater appreciation of the agencies and no longer believe that they are staffed by lazy bureaucrats. The White House was particularly gratified by this result, for if a day comes in which private enterprise cannot supply enough jobs, the public agencies will become far more important employers. However, this solution will be politically possible only if the general public looks favorably on government agencies.

Most of the employing agencies were pleased by the additional and free help they received, but some complained that incorporating part-timers for a few hours interfered with the work of the full-time workers or upset the organizational routine in other ways. Some CSWP workers performed poorly on the job, but others were so eager to work that they offered to put in extra hours for nothing. Most of *them* turned out to be workaholics.

The three-year test offered no answer for the main problem: the additional burden on the federal budget. Also, involuntary part-time workers were entitled to more than five to seven hours, and the unemployed were eligible for even more. However, CSWP is not organizationally equipped to place jobless people in full-time jobs or to duplicate the work of the agencies that now do so.

The most vocal opposition to CSWP, other than that from the defenders of the free market in labor, has come from a small group of utopians who welcome the shrinkage in work time. They believe that the federal government should institute a universal six hour day and twenty-four hour workweek as soon as possible, enabling people to devote the extra time to additional leisure, education, self improvement, culture, and other civilization enhancing activities. The Marxists added hunting and fishing to the list of pastimes, but they all agreed that the long dreamed of hope to liberate humankind from drudgery was now within reach.

Hernandez, who shared their beliefs when he was a young man, has welcomed their reaction. However, he also warned them that in the real world, working less and earning an insufficient income does not put people in the mood for new leisure time activities or the pursuit of culture. If they resorted to hunting and fishing, they would do so to reduce their grocery bills.

Hernandez also reminded the utopians that many of the machines once expected to do the work while people devoted themselves to enjoyment and enlightenment are now overseas, forcing Americans to work to pay for the products manufactured by those machines. For now, the utopian vision must remain just that.

CHAPTER THREE

MOVING TOWARD WORLD PEACE

AND PLANETARY SURVIVAL

On September 11, 2012, Jennifer Grant was in Los Angeles for some last minute fund-raising for the Caruso-Grant campaign and woke up feeling the floor of her hotel room shaking. After several more shocks, she got up and prepared herself for her first breakfast meeting. On her way back to Washington, she realized that only a couple of the many people she met that day had brought up the earthquake.

Months later, the cabinet was discussing terrorism. Recalling that day in Los Angeles, Grant reminded the group that the long predicted earthquake that would likely destroy large parts of California had never taken place. Moreover, once all possible preventive measures had been undertaken and forecasting mechanisms perfected, Californians essentially stopped thinking about earthquakes and went on with their lives.

Wasn't it time, she suggested, to think about applying the same reaction to terrorism? Despite the steady continuation of suicide bombings as well as other kinds of violent attacks on civilians in the Middle East and other parts of the world, another massacre on the scale of 9/11 had not occurred. Evidently no one so far had been able to summon up the personnel, planning, and money to carry out such an atrocity.

The United States had been even freer of such attacks. The few American incidents that could be called terroristic were carried out by nativist militias, drug sellers, and rival violent gangs, with no Arabs, Muslims, or other suspect "foreign" groups involved. The FBI regularly caught amateur groups who bragged about their plans but actually had none, and they also intercepted a few groups who did have plans but were easily apprehended before they could act. The FBI was on the trail of a few suspected professional terrorists who, as it turned out later, were looking for a commission from someone who wanted to attack America.

If Californians could avoid being obsessed with an earthquake that might never come, why would America not respond the same way to what were as of now hypothetical terrorists? The government would have to suggest this reaction calmly and confidently and demonstrate convincingly that the country's intelligence, surveillance, and counterterrorism forces were at work 24/7. If this approach was effective, the public might be able to ignore the politicians and generals who still sought to evoke and stoke public fear. Perhaps people would even realize how much they were terrorizing themselves with the possibility that 9/11 could happen again.

Caruso had, like others, harbored similar doubts about the country's actual danger from terrorism, and he was intrigued by Grant's earthquake analogy. Although no more a pacifist than Grant, he hoped he would never have to authorize a war, especially an unnecessary one. He was also learning that the country could no longer afford recurrent war making, even if it sometimes spurred short-term economic growth.

Still, Caruso was, like Grant, fully aware of the political dangers of questioning the threats of terrorism. The Republicans and some Democrats had played upon the public's insecurities, its demand for safety, and the moral opprobrium associated with appeasement. More important, even a small violent incident that could be connected, directly or indirectly, to Al Quaida, Communists, or other real and imagined enemies would destroy Caruso's ability to govern and might lead to his impeachment.

Consequently, Grant and Caruso said nothing more on this subject until the early discussions of the new federal budget several months later. Then, one pleasant spring weekend at Camp David, Caruso recounted Grant's original earthquake story and wondered how domestic, foreign, and defense policy could be altered if terrorism could be downgraded from a threat to an unlikely or even highly unlikely occurrence. Could plans for possible future wars, antiterrorism operations, and other military projects be rethought?

Once rumors surfaced that the White House was having second thoughts about terrorism, Caruso and Grant scheduled a TV discussion in California to present some of these questions to the country. Grant again told her LA story, Caruso asked the audience rhetorically if they ever thought about the big earthquake, and he presented a new White House poll that indicated that most did not.

The two leaders told their national audience that although they would end the "war" on terrorism and military activities justified by that war, they intended to keep America safe from terrorists. Surveillance and intelligence gathering programs to do so were in place, and enough military and police forces were always available to deal with violent attacks on civilians, if such occurred. The monies saved from downgrading military preparations and unnecessary homeland security practices would be reallocated to job creation and other forms of economic growth.

The White House nervously awaited the public response and was not surprised by it or by its intensity. The most emotional reactions, pro and con, came from the remaining relatives of 9/11 victims and from fearful people imagining Al Quaida operatives or other terrorists leaving a nuclear bomb in a suitcase in the center of their communities. Moreover, many Americans retained strong memories of 9/11 and attacks that had occurred in other parts of the world, and some were fearful about the risks Washington would incur by undertaking any real or even symbolic disarmament. As expected, conservative hard-liners accused Caruso of endangering the American people, and a few pundits did call for his impeachment.

But most Americans also wanted no more of war. The first polls were favorable, and subsequent ones more favorable yet, after which

Caruso and Grant held talks with foreign leaders and requested the Secretaries of State, Defense, and Security to schedule extra meetings with their equals all over the world, all to reassure still nervous Americans. While the Pentagon was determining which weapons programs and other costly ventures could be canceled, Congress held hearings to look over, and publicize, the country's intelligence gathering arrangements and the work of U.S. intelligence organizations with intelligence agencies the world over.

Today we know that the Caruso-Grant gamble paid off and the country's obsession with domestic terrorism was unnecessary as long as America and its allies kept watch overseas. Admittedly, all modern countries have made dramatic improvements in intelligence gathering and in data analysis. As a result, humans as well as computer programs are now able to connect dots about possible external threats that were not even visible before 9/11.

Nevertheless, Caruso's policy change succeeded in large part because over the years the number of unexpected violent incidents— or at least the kinds of incidents that upset Americans—has been slowly declining everywhere in the world. Experts believe that Al Quaida and the other principal terror wielding groups have encountered the same organizational and budgetary problems as peaceful social movements.

A new generation of leaders is rejecting international violence in favor of seeking political and cultural control of the countries in which they are operating. They also aim to replace autocracy and entrenched bureaucracy, once more raising hopes that the cultures of despair can finally be eliminated.

These leaders are being supported by international programs to create new educational and work opportunities in poor communities wherever terrorism is rife. The programs aim to reduce the number of people who think about becoming terrorists, which in turn will reduce the influence and credibility of terrorist leadership. However, the number of educated bombers is shrinking even faster. A respectable number apparently have decided that killing innocent people does not change the rest of the world; others have found more satisfaction in political and religious reform movements. Some have even completed their education and entered one of the professions.

Admittedly, bombings of various kinds, though generally of

small magnitude, still take place all over the world. However, they have largely been the work of homegrown militants or psychotics who have somehow evaded police and intelligence services.

Even so, some Americans, including a few members of Congress, still worry about rogue nuclear bombers. For this and other reasons, Congress was less prepared to take risks and initially supported only half of Caruso's proposed military cutbacks. Two years later, Caruso tried again and was successful in obtaining further cuts. Subsequently, he made several major defense policy speeches that indicated that America would not resort to preemptive or other unnecessary wars and that the military would not use violence that endangered civilians. He insisted that his administration was dedicated to life-enhancing rather than life-destroying programs, although he was also careful to add that as commander in chief, he could not rule out military action if national security actually demanded it.

Every speech was followed by accusations of weak-mindedness and appeasement from the usual suspects. However, the White House carefully monitored the response from the rest of the country, and after his 2016 election victory, Caruso asked for a sizable reduction in those military expenditures not necessary to prevent violence.

CUTTING BACK MILITARY ACTIVITIES

Although his political instincts told him to go slowly in reducing the defense budget and his advisers reminded him that the permanent war economy had long been impervious to change, Caruso really had no choice; he needed to find extra funds for his economic programs. He also needed the votes of the people who depended on these programs, and they outnumbered the voters benefiting from the permanent war economy. Nonetheless, Caruso's first defense budget reduction proposal fell flat, for weapons makers and other Pentagon supporters were mobilized in nearly every important congressional district to point out how many jobs would be lost by Caruso's cost cutting scheme.

Eventually, Caruso found some money by talking the Pentagon into putting off the new weapons systems that employed the fewest workers. Later, he met with his fellow heads of state to end further work on all missile defense systems. That enabled O'Hara to begin and Gordon to continue negotiations for an international agreement to terminate the development of new weapons systems. Hernandez has already picked up the ball from Gordon, but very few people believe that such an agreement will ever be reached.

In the meantime, the United States and other large nations had to fund the cyberspace defense program. Making sure that other nations could not sabotage the computers and software that all countries now need to function was, and remains, expensive, but as every president had to agree, no one was killed or wounded, directly at least, by this kind of warfare. Some years later, the Pentagon would brag that its cyberspace defense system could spin off technology to put an end to spam e-mail and other Internet spoilers.

Caruso and Gordon moved a bit more slowly in decreasing the number of troops. Troop reduction would not only add to unemployment but would deprive the country of an effective occupational training facility for young people unlikely to go to college. However, both Caruso and Gordon retained the so-called Rumsfeld policy by which many of the military's combat forces were reorganized into small special services groups that easily could be sent wherever they were needed.

As it turned out, none of the three presidents has had to fight wars even of the Iraq I or II scale, although Caruso participated in arranging the departure of the last American military personnel to leave Iraq. Caruso also had to help a friendly African dictator stay in power but was able to insist on a set of democratizing measures that subsequently led to her ouster. O'Hara withstood pressure to send U.S. special forces to intervene in an African border dispute. Gordon authorized one case of Central American regime change, but the regime was so unpopular that the American intervention was virtually bloodless.

By then, the remaining American big firms operating in Latin America were so desperate to preserve their remaining goodwill that they no longer dared to ask for Washington's political help. The White House also intervened quietly in a number of civil wars and prevented a few coups d'état but never on its own; it always participated in international efforts and received official or unofficial approval from the Security Council.

Of course, past world tensions have never quite disappeared. For example, both Caruso and Gordon got into what the pundits called pissing matches with the Russians over long-standing issues, including by now ancient nuclear warheads as well as Russian autocracy and its by-products. From time to time, conservatives demanded that Russia be required to behave like America's representative democracy, and Wall Street wanted it to play by the rules of American capitalism.

O'Hara was part of the Republican interventionist wing, but he was only slightly more eager than Caruso to send anyone to war. Actually, many military experts believed that traditional wars were becoming obsolete. Conflicts over boundaries had been settled for the moment, and only a few nations still needed land on which to park surplus populations. Even wars over scarce raw materials were less and less defensible since the materials themselves could be destroyed so easily. Oil fields could be bombed to bits, but no country wanted to be blamed for further reducing the world's oil supply.

Partly as a result, most of the century's wars so far have been civil wars of various kinds and magnitudes. Some involved struggles between two or more groups for control of the state. Others were conflicts between majorities and minorities—often powerless majorities fighting to throw off domination by minorities that had taken over with the help of colonial occupiers. The class and power struggles were often hidden behind fanatic ethnic and religious identities. However much they inflamed the fighting, for example, among the varieties of Muslims, the warring groups were usually moved by anger over a series of political or economic injustices and sometimes as a result of frustrated rising expectations for a more tolerable existence. A few struggles have been exceedingly brutal, but none have so far turned into large-scale genocides.

American military forces participated several times in UN-sponsored and other peacekeeping interventions in these civil wars and were involved less publicly in conflicts that threatened to become civil wars, mostly of course in countries that were allies or de facto American colonies and former colonies. The United States assisted in capturing the perpetrators of violent incidents and actual or imagined leaders of terrorist groups, and it prevented, as well as helped to carry out, a few assassinations. The CIA participated quietly in a handful of elections and also sabotaged a couple before the White House could stop it.

Most of the nondiplomatic activities were carried out by the special services forces operating out of the many small, and a few large, bases the United States still maintained all over the world. Caruso and Gordon were personally embarrassed by many of these activities, and they ended those that were patently illegal or immoral or hurt America's international reputation. Every so often, however, they were stuck; forbidding such activities might have resulted in more deleterious consequences than letting them continue. At times the presidents were not informed of the operations until it was too late to halt them. Much as they disliked doing so, they also had to protect their deniability.

At times, the two presidents both wanted to support rebels or minorities in the world's conflicts, but they discovered that as heads of a state, they were expected to support other states. The State Department was aptly named. Occasionally, the CIA and lesser known government intelligence agencies supported the democratic opposition, but they are still learning to nurture the needed democratic institutions.

Finally, bringing peace to Iraq had provided plenty of experience, good and bad, for future peacemaking. After several years of negotiation and with a large budget for population relocation and rehousing, the United Nations was able to obtain agreement on a partitioning scheme. The sticking point was Baghdad, the central parts of which finally became an international zone. The remaining areas were allocated to Iraqis and others who wanted to live in ethnic and religious diversity. The country's Sunni zone was small because of the Shia's years of often genocidal ethnic cleansing. Many observers thought that eventually the remaining Sunni would leave if America, or Saudi Arabia or other Sunni-dominated countries, invited them.

The Security Council had to take over the oil fields and has delegated their operation to a limited profit international consortium, which distributes the income from the oil fields directly to the Iraqi people. The governments of the former Iraq obtain the rest of their budgets from income and other taxes, but tax collection itself has been outsourced to foreign governments and private companies.

These not only are less likely to be corrupted but are also politically freer to be tough on tax dodgers. If their methods work, some people will suggest that they be hired to aid America's tax collectors.

ENDING UNNECESSARY WARS

When Caruso, Gordon, and Hernandez first met in New York, their bonding was hastened by their shared horror about the ease with which the White House could start wars. In a society of over 300 million people, a dozen or even fewer high level officials sometimes had the power to end or impair the lives of many thousands of Americans and millions of foreigners they designated as the country's enemies. The trio also talked about the immense cost of these wars. Over the years they regularly speculated about the improvements in people's lives they could have made with the trillions spent on war making.

True, the dozen instigators of war needed support from the Pentagon brass, many other leading officials, and eventually at least a sizable minority of the voters. However, ever since the second Iraq war turned into another quagmire, the voters' support for war making was on the decline. While few people other than the antiwar radicals of the period had questioned the number of American casualties during the Korean and Vietnam wars, even before the first Iraq conflict, wars resulting in such significant American casualties were no longer politically acceptable.

Although the total number of American dead in the two Iraq wars never reached even a tenth of the casualties in Vietnam, the national news media had from the start counted and named every single American who was killed or wounded. The problems of the wounded, as well as those coming home with war-induced traumatic disorders, eventually became newsworthy as well. By 2012, polls showed a large majority of Americans opposing further preemptive or preventive American war making, with a rising number of people unsure whether wars ever could be necessary or just. But by now, the World War II generation that could testify in favor of necessary wars was dying out fast.

Caruso and Grant decided that the popular mood justified a public discussion of just and unjust as well as necessary and unnecessary wars. The two leaders were agreed that just war was an oxymoron; no war was ever just to the civilians—and probably not to most soldiers either. Privately the two wondered for whom wars were ever just and whether wars were even necessary, but they wanted to avoid the political uproar from organized patriots and others if their doubts became public. Caruso was rescued by a young White House brainstormer who suggested that the public discussion assume that wars were unnecessary until proved otherwise, thus requiring the supporters of war to demonstrate their necessity.

Before the end of their second term, Caruso and Grant were emboldened to ask Congress for legislation opposing wars that could not be proved necessary for America's ascertainable short-run security and safety. Congress agreed only to discussing a resolution and before finally approving it added a clause that the resolution had to be reconsidered every two years. In addition, direct attacks on the country automatically voided the resolution.

The national debate quieted down during the O'Hara years, but when Gordon became president, she asked Congress to make the resolution against unnecessary war permanent. Her White House revised the resolution slightly, however, suggesting that wars were necessary only if the safety and security of the country and its people could not be protected in any other way.

The congressional debate was short, but it was fierce, for the hawks wanted to add the country's well-being to the resolution. The doves objected, pointing out that achieving America's well-being might justify an American war to control the planet's entire supply of oil. They also insisted that safety and security be limited to people and places inside the country's borders. This time, the doves won, and the permanent resolution passed, but the hawks assured themselves that a resolution could always be made moot if foreign events required America to go to war.

Moreover, Gordon was careful not to ask for a ban on military measures short of war, although most in the Congress knew that the special forces sometimes carried out warlike activities of various kinds. These activities all required White House approval, which Gordon sometimes wanted desperately to withhold but ultimately almost always had to give.

Subsequently, Gordon submitted a revised resolution that would require the decision to undertake war to be made democratically. Although she was loath to surrender any presidential power in principle, her vice president (General Richard Potter) and most of her cabinet secretaries opposed the right of one person, even if that person was the commander in chief, to initiate wars. Perhaps the president should not even be commander in chief.

Although the Constitution assigned the war making power to Congress, Gordon was not eager to give it sole responsibility. Congress caught war fever more easily than the White House, especially if the voters became feverish as well, and voters often caught the war bug at the start of war. Although hawks described their enthusiasm as democracy in action, Gordon believed that extended government deliberation, including consideration by the Supreme Court, was necessary, if only to remind the voters that feverish impulses for war regularly ignored long-term consequences that could endanger the country's health.

Eventually, Gordon and the Congress agreed that presidents should make the proposal to go to war but that the actual decision to go to war should be reached in two stages. Assuming the first vote was positive—and no president would propose war if he or she expected a congressional rejection—the second vote would occur a week after the first. This time, congressional approval required a two-thirds vote of all members of both the House and the Senate and a supportive decision by the U.S. Supreme Court. Presidents were given the right to set aside the second vote and, with the Court's approval, even the first stage if America was under attack or for other genuine emergencies.

Later, Gordon suggested that in the future, national polls on the question should be conducted before each congressional vote, but arguments over the reliability and validity of and the democratic rationale for such momentous polls are still going on now, nearly five years after she made her suggestion.

Gordon also believed that if war making was to be democratized, the draft should be reinstated. If and when Americans were being asked to risk their lives in a war, the risk should be shared as widely as possible. However, Congress would not go along, and Hernandez has already indicated that he hopes the draft will not be needed while he is in the White House.

Radical Questions

The debate over necessary wars was accompanied by a yet more radical questioning of war: young people asking why they should be asked to give up or ruin their lives in war unless it was demonstrably necessary for the survival of the country. They could not understand why so many parents let their children be killed, especially when their deaths resulted from friendly fire, strategic and organizational mistakes, or interservice rivalries.

This discussion quickly transcended old ideological divides of conservatives and liberals, as well as those of hawks and doves. For example, some young conservatives wanted to know why they were supposed to give up their lives or their health to a government whose domestic policies they opposed and that they sought to shrink in favor of further individual rights.

Liberals asked why their lives should be put at risk unless the country was actually and immediately endangered. Defending the nation or its honor was hard to justify, since the nation was merely a set of loyalties, symbols, and other imaginaries that could not experience honor and that had not always been honorable. Protecting something as unspecified and commercialized as the American way of life seemed even more unjustifiable. Older people spoke of the destruction of lives and societies caused by Hitler, Stalin, Mao, Idi Amin, Saddam Hussein, and others, but their argument carried little weight with young people for whom George W. Bush had been the most dangerous leader on the planet.

The Case for Regime Change

In some ways the most original contribution to antiwar thought came from a group calling itself pragmatic pacifists that wanted to know why countries had to be destroyed and civilians and soldiers killed in order to persuade their governments to change policies or leaders. They called for regime change as a substitute for war and favored kidnappings and even assassinations of leaders if warlike regimes could not be changed peacefully or their leaders encouraged to go into exile. The group emphasized that it considered these measures unacceptable in themselves and supported them only as a replacement for war, as the lesser of two evils.

Thus, the pragmatic pacifists asked whether more attempts to depose or kill Saddam Hussein could not have taken place before the second Iraq war and why the bombing of Nazi headquarters in Berlin and equivalent locations in Tokyo would not have been more appropriate than the total destruction of German and Japanese cities. They could not begin to understand why the United States did not bomb the rail lines and roads to the Nazi concentration camps or why Truman allowed the atomic bombing of Hiroshima and Nagasaki instead of dropping a tiny such bomb in the gardens of the emperor's palace. Some assumed that this American president must have been criminally insane.

Such reactions seem particularly relevant in an era in which most national intelligence agencies have identified the offices, residences, and resting and hiding places of the world's leaders. Moreover, military aircraft can now drop pinpoint bombs on the leaders, these days perhaps without even harming their bodyguards.

Admittedly, regime change in lieu of war would not work in countries in which war-making leaders have widespread popular support, but if it is possible to depose those leaders, their successors would not necessarily continue the same murderous policies. Leaders with strong army backing would be harder to remove, but perhaps monetary or other incentives could sometimes persuade the army to support a more peaceful leader. Many soldiers would probably have preferred such a leader in the first place.

Others were asking the next, and more difficult, round of questions: which regime, or who in it, had the right to decide to remove another regime or its leaders, on what grounds, and at what point? More important, how could and why should regime change itself guarantee that the new regime would be peaceful and democratic?

Scholars of war came up with other searching questions: for example, whether and how regime change could stop wars undertaken because of geopolitical and other power imbalances and vacuums. And who would dare undertake regime change in a superpower that could retaliate with all-out war? The Democracy Project think tank wanted to know why the voters could not be asked to choose between regime change and war.

Gordon and her colleagues listened closely and sympathetically to the public debate on regime change, sometimes finding it hard not to participate, but they studiously avoided any official or even on-deep-background comments from unnamed senior White House officials. Not long after the debate started, Gordon issued a brief statement indicating that she was hearing what was being said but that national security concerns required her to be silent. She would speak only if and when a national consensus was in the offing.

However, Gordon never spoke, and now the ball is in Hernandez's court. It is rumored that he wants to raise the regime change question but believes that the political risks are too great, especially since he, like his predecessors, will be meeting and negotiating with national leaders who might be targets for regime change. Nonetheless, regime change remains preferable if it could spare the world another war.

Internationalizing War Criminals

Beginning with the unsuccessful attempt to send the Bush administration's instigators of the second Iraq war to stand trial in the Hague, the world's antiwar movements have proposed expanding trials of war criminals to include the responsible elected and appointed leaders among the victors. Expecting immediate protests from world leaders who might someday have to take their country to war against their will, the supporters of this policy indicated that they would initially favor limiting the trials to leaders who initiated unnecessary wars. Some advocated adding national leaders, as well as ministers and generals who have been directly responsible for the unnecessary killing of soldiers and civilians alike.

The antiwar movements noted further that individual leaders, civilian and military, were rarely responsible by themselves for decisions to go to war or for the brutality of war. Thus, extenuating circumstances and larger causes had to be considered before leaders were accused of criminal acts. Still, if wars were ever to be eliminated, eventually all national leaders had to be potentially subject to being tried.

Hernandez is said to be ambivalent. On the one hand, this proposal would enable him and his successors to resist domestic political pressures to go to war. On the other hand, world courts might criminalize individual leaders unfairly. Perhaps the ideal solution would have each nation prosecute its own leaders. Although few nations could be expected to do so, except after an extremely unpopular or disastrous war, the threat of prosecution might add yet another disincentive to war making.

Meanwhile, a lively public debate has ensued over the eligibility requirements for war criminals. In order to support this debate, a group of military historians has put together a historical list of war criminal candidates. Their list goes far back into history, is very long, and includes a number of leaders who then became national heroes and a few who were even deified.

The historians also estimated the number of soldiers and innocent civilians each candidate had killed intentionally or otherwise. Since the greatness of civilizations traditionally has been measured in part by their success in war making, the historians' work has encouraged a reevaluation of the idea of civilization. If keeping the peace or at least avoiding unnecessary war and brutality is a relevant criterion, Homo sapiens has so far created only a small handful of civilizations.

ENHANCING UN PEACEKEEPING

At the start of the twenty-first century, UN peacekeeping was frequently oxymoronic: its peacekeepers were unable to act even as battles and atrocities took place in front of them. Since this state of affairs could not last without eventually destroying the peacekeepers' and even the United Nations' credibility, the peacekeepers themselves finally urged that the Security Council and General Assembly give them authority to engage in limited combat if necessary.

The two bodies took years to provide that authority, partly because member states did not want to threaten their alliances by burdening their warring allies with peacekeepers. As a result, the UN peacekeepers have too often not been allowed to keep the peace. When the United Nations began to be seen as a laughingstock, the two bodies tried unsuccessfully to disqualify member states with such alliances from participating in peacekeeping decisions. Then, in desperation, the Secretary General was given unilateral authority to choose and send peacekeepers wherever they were needed.

The Secretary General has used her authority with all due political care. As a result, the peacekeepers' effectiveness is increasing slowly but surely, and the Secretary General can exercise economic and other sanctions when the peacekeepers encounter undue interference. UN peacekeeping has also turned into an employment program of sorts, some member countries volunteering additional peacekeeping troops and material aid for that reason. Others have even shared some results of their intelligence gathering. As a result, the United Nations currently has more choice of personnel and also more experience in selecting the most appropriate peacekeepers for the countries and situations in which these must operate.

The peacekeepers have done less well in areas and countries experiencing civil wars, having frequently been under orders or pressure to support the party that controls the state. Consequently, rebel and other oppositional forces have objected, and when they have been supported by nations on the Security Council, the peacekeepers have been immobilized. Since many peacekeeping assignments involve civil wars, the United Nations will have to find a way to transcend power politics so that the peacekeepers can control violence by both or all sides.

Above all, the Security Council must be able to prevent member nations allied with warring nations or civil war participants from sabotaging UN efforts. Their interference has declined over the years, but the United Nations still lacks the power to restrain or punish the world's superpowers. World opinion can be called on occasionally, but international economic and power politics still trump that opinion.

The pressure on the United Nations is all the greater because antiwar movements and others influencing world opinion have already talked about someday transferring most or all of the world's peacekeeping to the United Nations. The Security Council and its allies hope that such a transfer would help reduce incentives for war. If the United Nations assumes a greater role in peacekeeping, member states might be able to reduce their military budgets.

Beyond Peacekeeping

In the last few years, the United Nations has been asked to assist in the involuntary movements of large numbers of people who, as a result of civil war or catastrophe, generally end up in new refugee camps. However, UN and other study groups are already considering long-range plans for how and where to locate people who will have to move if global warming and flooding make their present homes uninhabitable. Fortunately, massive and involuntary population movements are probably still decades away, for right now no country wants a large number of involuntary newcomers and neither the United Nations nor anyone else has figured out how to persuade nations with habitable but virtually empty regions to make them available to the victims of global warming or other disasters.

In addition, the Security Council has talked informally about the possibility of population movements in areas where oppositional groups and even nations are fighting over the same piece of land. Such movements are most necessary in areas in which too many people occupy too little land.

These population movements would have to be voluntary and would in any case depend on the willingness and ability of stricken or warring nations to give up their populations and receiving countries to admit the refugees. Few countries are eager to lose populations, unless they are pariah groups or threats to the regime. And although some of the many low fertility countries need more young people, they are reluctant to admit poor ones, especially the politically militant, as well as those with different skin colors.

So far, the decanting policy, as it is called, is being tested in simulation studies, and the populations and countries being studied remain an official secret. Still, migration specialists assume that several poverty stricken and overpopulated countries are under examination as are areas of religious and ethnic conflict, as well as those that have absorbed refugees of war and natural disaster.

The currently most controversial study, the existence of which is firmly denied, involves Israel and Palestine. UN area experts believe that population pressures endanger the futures of both states. If the experts are correct that the two states have more people than their lands and economies can support, the danger of violent political conflict is never going to be totally eradicated. In that case, some voluntary outmigration from both states might offer a partial solution.

The United States is usually first on the study list of potential receiving countries and might be agreeable to receiving some Israelis and Palestinians. The American Jewish community is shrinking in size, the Arab American community wants to grow, and both may have enough political clout to get their wish. Questions that are controversial both politically and in other ways need to be answered first: Which Israelis and Palestinians want to come? Which ones will the American subcommunities accept? And which ones will the United States actually admit?

White Americans worried about the country's growing Latino population might be receptive to immigrants perceived as white if increases in antisemitism and anti-Arab prejudice can be kept to a minimum. However, no one wants advocates of war, sectarian violence, or militant nationalism or members of apocalyptic religions, even if they or their children might become less threatening once they moved to America.

Optimistic Middle East experts believe that sufficient decanting might increase the possibility of Israel and Palestine eventually merging into a single binational state. More realistic observers want to know why nationalist fires in each state should cool and how enough religious and cultural convergence could take place to make a binational state feasible. Would economic growth be sufficient to bring about a decline in Palestinian fertility to make sure that the two populations will be roughly equal in size?

Hernandez may be asked to join the leaders of other nations to make the simulation studies public and to urge the Security Council to consider decanting as a partial solution of last resort especially if and when genocide or ethnic cleansing threatens. At the end of the Vietnam war, the military brought the Hmong to America to prevent their being killed by the victorious North Vietnamese. The Hmong were few in number, and too many have remained poor too long in the United States, but the overall effectiveness of the resettlement might serve as a model for similar deliberate population movements.

THE UNITED NATIONS AS PEACEMAKER

The world's rising opposition to war has naturally elevated expectations for world peace, resuscitated older social movements advocating world government, and put pressure on the United Nations to move beyond peacekeeping to peacemaking. Some internationalists believe that eventually the United Nations should establish autonomous military and intelligence services, perhaps recruited through a worldwide draft and paid for by a tax on the world's nations as well as on its global business organizations. There are even people who believe that someday such a United Nations could authorize and carry out regime changes to prevent wars and civil wars. However, these people are almost everywhere described as hopelessly utopian.

The experts doubt that the Security Council members would give up their veto and other powers and that many General Assembly nations would approve arming an international body that has not so far excelled in self-government. And the dictators of the world have enough commonalities of interest to prevent democratic nations from restraining them.

Others, especially the more fervent internationalists, believe the idea is worth thinking about. As they see it, the United Nations might be able to exert authority over small countries and try to make peace in their wars and civil wars. It probably could not restrain the superpowers, but it might embarrass them out of undertaking some warlike ventures. Perhaps it could even settle minor conflicts between them.

The internationalists also claim that a stronger United Nations should be able to organize, with regional unions and other large bodies, a new attack on the inequality of what remains, after all these years, the third or developing world. Perhaps it could also discourage exploitation of this world by the multinational and multicontinental corporations.

In a more distant future, the United Nations might have to become the dominating multicontinental, allocating some of the world's scarcest resources across national boundaries. At the same time, however, it would also need to turn into a monstrously large government. If and when the now expected crises and catastrophes of global warming begin, it would be the logical body to coordinate a defense against rising oceans as well as flooding, overheating, and freezing land masses. Someday, the United Nations might also be the only body able to exert some control over the population movements that will be necessary to prevent genocidal battles over the declining amount of habitable territory. At that point, sheer planetary necessity might send it on its way to becoming a world government.

GLOBAL ENERGY AND GLOBAL WARMING

When Caruso decided to run for president, the country had accepted the reality of global warming, although not many were willing or able to do much to attack its causes. As always, the educated middle class, which had both the ideological inclination to act on this new knowledge and the financial ability to make the necessary lfestyle changes, made the first moves. Just as it had initiated the aerobic exercise habit, watched its trans fat consumption, and purchased organic food, it now was first in line to buy fluorescent lightbulbs and, in lesser numbers, to install solar panels. It was also ready to sign petitions to rein in the oil and coal industries and support green movements of all kinds.

Other Americans would follow the lead of this middle class at their own pace, and eventually their number would grow—although for many years there would be some Americans who still did not want to hear about global warming. Few, even in the upper middle class, realized that their well meant efforts were mere tokens that made them feel better but did little to actually reduce the magnitude of harmful emissions. Not many people were yet prepared to consider that drastic alterations in their everyday lives might someday be necessary.

Once the Caruso administration came into office, it was immediately confronted with the more pressing problem of the moment: the rising world demand for and the resulting ever higher cost of oil. Like other politicians all over the world, Caruso had to keep the gasoline flowing into drivers' gas tanks and the oil into their furnaces—and as cheaply as possible. Even dictators found it impossible to ignore driver protests when gas became scarcer or more costly. In rapidly industrializing countries, affluent drivers who were concurrently discovering the comforts of home heating and cooling only added to the demand for oil, coal, and natural gas.

As a result, some members of the administration were worried about the possibility of future oil wars among countries trying to obtain control over major oil fields in politically weak countries. No one would attack the United States for its oil, but many Asian, African, and Latin American nations had more than enough under-employed peasants for massive armies to march on the nearest oil fields. One party states might risk an oil war to keep their car-owning citizens content enough not to endanger the party's control.

Occasionally, even Americans, including lobbyists speaking for manufacturing firms and automobile owners, urged that the United States take over the Latin American, African, or Arabian oil fields. Some historians unwittingly supported their arguments by reinterpreting the Iraq wars as the first oil wars, and the advocates of a new round of such wars argued that the government had learned enough from the mistakes made in Iraq to undertake another oil war.

Few people who had voted for Caruso supported such thinking, and the White House, still guilty over the country's failure to sign the Kyoto antiwarming agreement, had different priorities. It wanted to join with other countries to speed up the production of substitutes for oil and other fossil fuels and persuade people to reduce their energy usage. Fortunately, this would also contribute to the reduction of global warming.

Unfortunately, however, the politicians, in America as elsewhere, had to overcome formidable political obstacles. First, people who were totally dependent on and could not long exist without oil and other fossil fuels wanted assurance that their needs would be met without interruption before they would support politicians who proposed life-changing programs to reduce global warming.

Second, many people—other than those who had already lived through level 4 and 5 hurricanes—expected little harm to the planet in their lifetimes and perhaps even those of their children and were not prepared to look further ahead. Some were probably in early denial, but others said they could not think about the fate of descendants they would never know.

Only those who already had grandchildren and great-grandchildren worried about their futures. And many people believed that neither they nor the country needed to resort to drastic or expensive changes until the predicted dangers of global warming actually materialized.

Elected officials and the industries that produced energy were aware of people's feelings. However, the politicians also had to keep the possibility in mind that the harmful effects of global warming, or at least those directly affecting their constituents, would come earlier than expected. In that case, they would be blamed for not having acted sooner. On the other hand, the projections of future global warming could be proved wrong, and then they would be blamed for having imposed unnecessary programs.

Third, at the moment, the only immediately viable substitute for oil was ethanol, which had already been mixed with gasoline for years but was at least as expensive as oil. If new oil reserves were found and the price of oil crashed, the voters could surely demand a slowdown in the energy conversion process and lose interest in substitutes for fossil fuels.

Worse yet, the world had endless supplies of coal, which was cheaper than oil but also spewed more carbon dioxide into the atmosphere than all other fuels and would only increase global warming. Moreover the coal companies, eager to mine and sell their coal, were also marketing liquified coal. They advertised the virtues of what they called the coal bargain, and enough drivers and homeowners were ready to take the bargain even if that could result in a more polluted atmosphere later.

Someday, coal's carbon emissions could perhaps be trapped and rendered harmless. Long-lasting electric batteries to run cars, nuclear energy that was neither risky nor produced nuclear waste, and other technological fixes that actually helped cool the atmosphere might be available too. But many of the solutions being tried out in the laboratory would not work in the real world, and others would not be ready for a long time. By then people might already have learned how to live at lower energy levels.

Fourth, the efforts of one country to reduce global warming could continue to be offset by the unwillingness or inability of others to do so. Some countries would be able to free ride, benefiting from the efforts of their neighbors without paying costs other than international scorn. However, no country or agency had enough political or economic power to make others do their share. And the poorer countries, some of which were also among the biggest polluters, could not afford to do other than free ride.

These and other political problems notwithstanding, toward the end of the second decade of the century, as TV showed the world its ever faster melting glaciers, the world's democratic leaders knew they had to act more quickly to slow down global warming and dangerous emissions. Caruso and Grant spent a lot of time in the last years of their administration pointing out that someday America's dependence on cars might have to be reduced in favor of some form of mass transit and that the next generation of Americans could be living and working at higher density. (These changes are spelled out in chap. 5, "Family, Home, and Community.")

Changing Energy Lifestyles

Creating new energy sources, whether through biomass farming, harnessing the sun and the wind, or inventing technologies, has been beset with unexpected problems. Nonetheless, it has been far easier than getting people to alter energy-dependent habits and institutions. America and the newly rich countries are most addicted to car use, and people have continued to drive virtually as much as before even when gasoline, whether made out of oil, coal, or cellulose, costs $10 a gallon or more.

True, Americans have had little choice; most are used to low density living in a largely low density country where in some areas mass transit alternatives are primitive or unavailable, especially west of the Mississippi River. However, as mentioned in chapter 1 ("2033 and Before"), vehicles have become much smaller. In addition, people have cut back significantly on Sunday drives and vacation trips, and the modern world's privileged adolescents went into mourning as many parents took away their cars or driving privileges and bought them bicycles.

Caruso had occasionally raised the need for a carbon tax during the 2012 election campaign, but he stopped when the TV and Internet ads became so vicious that they upset too many drivers and homeowners who normally voted Democratic. Once elected, Caruso and Grant mentioned the tax in some of their joint talks, and after the 2014 election, Caruso sent a bill to Congress that proposed both a carbon tax on consumers and what he called a health charge on energy producing firms whose products contributed most heavily to global warming.

Congress was delighted to be able to vote down the carbon tax and endorse the health fee, especially since it would be paid by firms, not by voters. True, the firms would pass on the costs, and many prices would rise once more, but as always, most consumers only grumbled about price increases while many protested against higher taxes of any kind. Years later, when a significant number of illnesses and deaths could be attributed to temperature increases and emissions, a carbon tax became politically feasible even as the health fees continued to rise.

Partly as a result of the increasing impact of global warming on everyday life, reducing the size of cars and increasing the efficiency of their engines has turned out to be easier than in the past. That an ever smaller number of giant car companies are building the world's vehicles has helped too, for despite the companies' economic power, they are dependent on the world's governments, which can now virtually determine the price of whatever liquid goes into everyone's gas tanks.

Many if not most Americans, at least in the more densely built up areas of the country, now drive hybrid mini cars, and by the mid 2020s, sub-minis were sold for short commutes to work and trips to the mall. Some engineers are already inventing or reinventing sub-sub minis, including three wheelers, and motorized bicycles are replacing motorcycles. Some comics claim that as cars shrink in size, drivers and passengers will have to do likewise. Perhaps the automobile industry will enable Americans to eliminate obesity-related health problems.

Even the engineers cannot solve a fundamental problem associated with very small cars: they do not have room for the entire family. They can hold two people comfortably for journeys to work and errand running, but four people can be squeezed into them only for very short trips. Consequently, families with more than one child still want something larger than a sub-mini.

A second insoluble problem: what if a really long lasting battery that needs only weekly or biweekly charging is invented? Then many Americans might buy larger cars again and force some small car builders of the world into bankruptcy. The various mass transit projects now being planned or under way could face sudden death or at least a significant slowing.

For the moment, however, and with smallness very much "in," the original Detroit automobile industry now has a virtual monopoly on building big cars, most of which actually are midsized by earlier twenty-first-century standards. Indeed, the remaining American car companies flourish because they continue to build such big cars and even some giant ones, including SUVs and stretch limousines for the world market.

The main customers for big cars are America's westerners and people in other countries who must travel long distances to get to work and are prepared to pay the special weight taxes the federal government and other nations are finally able to levy on them. Rich entrepreneurs who feel a need to show off their economic heft buy the giant cars, as do dictators, but elected politicians, celebrities, entertainers, and the remaining royals have discovered that their constituents want to see them in small cars.

Still, the major customers for giant cars are the American jitney companies that have sprung up to help meet the increasing demand for mass transit in areas without anything more than the sparsest bus services. However, by the 2020s, when the federal government had used carrots and sticks to initiate a mass transit system that would someday span the nation, American car companies and others started to mass-produce electric and other busses.

Although most nations increased gasoline taxes steeply in order to cut down on driving, the concurrently rising price of gas created sufficient political protest to force politicians to cap the tax increases. Then the world's energy ministers had to take the next step: requiring drivers to cut their driving speeds to save fuel, money, and of course the world's atmosphere.

Admittedly the speeds common at the start of the twenty-first century are long gone. In America, speed limits on most highways, other than in the lowest density states, were reduced to fifty miles per hour in the early 2020s, although a number of elected officials, including governors, lost their jobs as a result.

Getting people to drive more slowly was immensely difficult, even when their commutes were short or they were working short weeks. Everyone was so used to reaching their destinations as fast as possible that slowing down was as difficult as stopping smoking. More difficult, in fact, because smoking could be controlled medically and by peer pressure, while highways are designed with the assumption that everyone is willing to drive at approximately the same speed.

At first, car design experiments were conducted to make speeding more difficult or uncomfortable by accelerator adjustments and by obligatory governors, most of which failed to survive the political process—or the drivers' ability to disconnect them. Gordon's reelection campaign panicked when her opponents brought up the so-called Governor governor, based on her brief advocacy of the mechanism while she was governor of Florida. By now, most countries outside the third world have automated enforcement of speed limits by photographing drivers' license plates with computers built into either road beds or traffic lights. Political battles over the size of the tickets for exceeding speed limits are endemic.

In the mid-2020s, several European countries began to lower highway speed limits to forty miles per hour or even less, but America's politicians have not yet dared to do so. Hernandez may risk it after the 2034 election, at least if his approval ratings hold up. However, he is also considering passing part of the buck to the states, letting those containing wide open spaces set their own speed limits. Hernandez may even propose that the states determine the weight taxes that now discourage the purchase of big cars. Perhaps the more densely populated regions of the country will then proceed with a further reduction of the speed limit.

The federal government is now undertaking studies of the slowdown effect to determine how the reduction in driving speed has affected other aspects of daily life. Psychiatrists are being surveyed to check whether traffic slowdowns increase road rage and other mental disorders or whether they lead to more relaxed overall lifestyles and improvements in mental health.

At the same time, a number of amusement park operators have earned millions by building tracks or renting obsolete bits of highway on which people can drive at the old speeds for a short while or take a turn around the park in ancient SUVs and Rolls Royces. In addition, auto racing has grown into a more popular spectator sport than it ever has been in the past.

The seemingly drastic measures to reduce automobile fuel consumption are necessary because the modern economy cannot run without large trucks, which probably will always use substantial amounts of carbon dioxide emitting fuel. Trucks will remain essential even when freight railroads can reach most parts of most countries—as they will soon again be able to do even in the United States. Airplanes will likewise remain essential to long distance domestic and international travel, especially if tourism becomes an ever more important economic base all over the world.

Furthermore, America and the other countries that are making significant reductions in carbon emission cannot win the battle against global warming until the modernized Asian nations, especially China and India, require their factories to meet the American and European emission standards. In addition, the leaders of these countries still have to figure out how to persuade their citizens not to waste electricity. Many still treat their air conditioners and furnaces as novelties and punish politicians who interfere with the temperature of their homes.

Meanwhile, a number of Americans are wearying of further environmental lifestyle adjustments. Journalists everywhere report people and communities failing to achieve their anti–global warming quotas. Republican politicians considering a run against Hernandez in 2036 grumble about foreign nations spoiling the planet for the American way of life.

CHAPTER FOUR

FIGHTING FOR FAIRNESS

Toward the end of Caruso's years in the White House, the long-term increase in income inequality had finally come to a halt, and during the next decade, the first signs of greater income equality have appeared. Caruso's jobs programs grew sufficiently during the Gordon years to have a visible effect on income distribution, but the various new taxes, the spread of the living wage, and other income programs have helped as well. Further progress can be expected once the wealth tax is fully operational. Some political observers hope political inequality will decline as well, although most people doubt that corporate and wealth taxes would significantly reduce the political clout of the very rich.

Still, more economic equality between the upper middle, median, and below median income populations might reduce class differences and their harshness somewhat. Occasional signs of a little more consensus and social harmony are already evident. If the lack of self-respect, stress, and clinical depression known to be associated with perceived inferiority would lessen, greater wealth and income equality could even produce a mentally healthier society. Most likely, even rising rates of economic and other equalities will have this effect; if people believe conditions are improving and the future looks brighter, they might even try a little harder to brighten it yet further.

However, America is not becoming an egalitarian society or a society of equals. Although the polls indicate people's lip service to equality, pursuing it has never been a popular political cause in America. Consequently, people will still be competing for more than their share of the scarce resources, for limited social positions, and for moves up the power and status ladders of everyday life. Although an ever smaller number may expect to grow rich, they nonetheless want a little more income than the people to whom they compare themselves. Even the poor seek to keep their distance from the desperately poor. But everyone from top to bottom strives to avoid downward mobility.

For this and other reasons, Caruso and Gordon almost never used the word *equality,* nor did Hernandez in his presidential campaign. The trio did not even admit that their many economic policies to improve the fortunes of the below median income population reflected an egalitarian agenda. Instead, they advocated their policies as the best path to economic growth.

When Caruso needed a substitute term for equality, he chose *fairness,* reminding his audiences of twentieth-century president Harry Truman's Fair Deal and the liberal twentieth-century concept of fair shares. Thereafter, fairness became a basic theme of Democratic economic and other policies.

ANTIPOVERTY POLICY

Caruso was even more reluctant to talk about poverty. The poor did not vote enough, and too many of them were dark skinned, as a result of which many better off Americans were against the poor as much as against poverty. If the economy could be maneuvered to provide enough decent jobs, many poor people would soon escape poverty with only minimal additional help. In that case, government needed mainly to help those who were in temporary need and those who were unable to work. Consequently, Caruso preferred, both by inclination and for political reasons, more general policies that helped others as well as the poor, especially others with a bit more political clout. That preference had always been one reason for his concern with below median income Americans.

In addition, Caruso felt that too much talk about poverty put unnecessary emphasis on the differences between the poor and the nonpoor. Until the economy was fixed, the best he could do was to talk about reducing those differences, and that began with reviving an old attempt to change the official definition of poverty. The government's poverty line, which dated back to the 1960s, stipulated an absolute amount of money that would assure people's physical survival, but it had long been set too low to achieve its stated aim.

Caruso, or rather his poverty experts, some of whom had grown up below that line, wanted to redefine poverty as the inability to afford the American standard of living. Instead of spelling it out they used data on how much money below median income American households felt they needed to afford the necessities, in goods and services, everyone else was getting.

Then, the most widely mentioned amount would be set as a poverty point, demarcating the minimal standard of living below which the poor should not fall. That point turned out to be 67 percent of the median family income, and Caruso proposed that for now, the government commit itself to bringing everyone to at least 60 percent of that median. The Republicans claimed the country could afford only 40 percent, and the Democratic majority in Congress settled on 50 percent, to be raised to 60 percent in the next four years.

The poverty floor was now officially raised by several thousand dollars, and it rose further in good economic times when the median income also rose. The new, higher poverty point also increased the number of poor, enabling the Republicans to blame the Democrats for increasing poverty in America.

Antipoverty legislation has always been slow to pass, and even the definitional change was not made until Caruso's second term. It might have been delayed further without America's Storekeepers, who campaigned for it to help themselves and the economy to sell more goods. But the new definition of poverty was still a definition, and the higher poverty point it established did not automatically lead to more jobs or higher incomes for the people now below that point. That would be accomplished largely by the income and jobs policies for healing the economy and the spread of the living wage described in chapter 2, "Healing the Economy."

Of course, the economy that shrunk poverty could also add to it, newly poor people being created when low wage industries moved overseas or declined and when employers in other industries cut work hours. At one point, Gordon sought unsuccessfully to float another earmark scheme, this one limited to projects and workplaces that would only hire newly poor workers.

The Survival Aid Program

Despite his opposition to formal antipoverty policies, Caruso was eventually talked into several. The first was a popular move; it terminated what little was left of "welfare." Instead he proposed three new programs, none of which included the term *welfare*. These programs were called "Survival Aid," "Parenting Help," and "Escape."

The Survival Aid Program (SAP) was blindingly simple: it would quickly supply modest financial aid to everyone who needed immediate help but was unable to obtain it from family or other sources, including banks. Applicants would have to offer some readily obtainable proof that they were dependent on government for their survival and then provide more proof a month later if the survival payments were still needed. They would also be expected to find work or choose a job from those offered. They could stay on SAP for a total of six months, although after that, further SAP payouts would be treated as minimal interest loans. Except in truly special cases, SAP loans would end after a year.

SAP's help is not entirely financial. Sometimes its staff obtains emergency day care when children are sick and parents are threatened with job loss if they do not go to work. SAP digs up loaner cars so people can get to work, and at times it can even commandeer emergency housing for the suddenly homeless.

SAP is popular because it trusts people in emergencies; is not laden with punitive rules; and, above all, also helps people who are not poor. Still, Congress was initially fearful of the cost of the program, reduced the amount of individual payouts Caruso had suggested, capped the total to be spent annually, and approved the program for only two years. Many public officials and others were worried that recipients would take advantage of the government, but evidently having to repay federal loans scared off all but some professional thieves.

The O'Hara administration did not approve of SAP, however, and left it near dead from underfunding. A few of the richer states took it over, but in 2025, the Gordon administration revived it, and Hernandez announced before his inauguration that it will continue while he is president.

Parenting Help

Caruso's second replacement for welfare offered financial help to those who had long been its major clients, poor single parents, most of them mothers, who could not work sufficiently to support their children or who were working long hours that endangered their ability and energy for parenting. Caruso felt that they too deserved help, and partly because he had promised not to target the poor, he also asked for assistance for better off mothers who had become single parents of young children and needed only temporary financial support.

Gordon was particularly interested in helping single parents. Some of her poverty experts thought single parents should stay home and take care of their children full-time until they were ready for nursery school or kindergarten. However, others believed that unless single parents had two or more young children, they should be able to work part-time, if only for their own self-respect. Since children were involved, Congress was prepared to be supportive but hoped that as more jobs were created and male unemployment declined, single mothers who wanted to marry would find men able and willing to be breadwinners and fathers.

Even so, the total number of single parents is not declining, for with the rise in singles, described in chapter 5, "Family, Home, and Community," single parents are more numerous than in the past. Most are employed and self-supporting, however, although some occasionally need emergency help.

The Escape Program

The Escape program sought to enable people to escape poverty, but the title notwithstanding, it is also a storage program for poor people who, even with all possible help, are unable to escape from poverty. The majority are people emotionally and physically unable to earn a living. Many have grown up in abusive or otherwise damaged families; are themselves damaged; and are often raising children, some of whom will end up being damaged. For centuries, many countries, including the United States, had called them society's dregs, but in the latter part of the twentieth century, the term *underclass* became popular. The anthropologist Hylan Lewis had more accurately described them as the clinical poor.

The Caruso administration and its successors have tried once more to help, protect, and control those who have been trapped in poverty. Some individuals only need to escape the people and institutions that have brought them bad luck. In fact, one experiment placed people in need of help in an adapted version of the witness protection program, trained them in new skills, and offered housing in a new community. Those who cannot be helped are considered disabled, receive disability benefits, and are eligible to turn to the Survival program in case of crises.

However, the children of the people in the Escape program have received the most attention, and it is their escape that the program is really seeking. Child saving programs have been tried for centuries, and in the past, children were removed from their families for this purpose. Today, children are thought to be better off with their parents unless these are directly and openly destructive. However, when possible, the children are sent to schools and after school programs in other neighborhoods, in part to distance them from the local street culture when it discourages an escape from poverty.

Many of the youngsters are bright, eager, and hopeful, and the right kind of extrafamilial supports enable a sizable proportion to escape. Persuading them at an early age that they can have a hopeful future if they work hard is important, but being there to help them achieve that future when they cannot do it on their own is even more important. However, too many cannot break away enough from familial and neighborhood networks; others find parental pathologies or other residuals of familial poverty catching up with them in adolescence or adulthood. Recidivism is greatest during economic downturns when crises associated with poverty are most likely to return.

EQUALITY FOR NONWHITES

Caruso's stance on racial equality was firm; he planned to say as little as possible and instead quietly to do as much as possible. Few white Americans now admit to racial intolerance, but they still remain more tolerant in opinion than in action. They seem to have no trouble supporting institutions and policies that keep racial minorities separate and unequal, especially if the minorities are African Americans.

Caruso had learned this lesson as a child, when he was told how his poor Sicilian ancestors were discriminated against as blacks and had been called guineas. The family skin brightened as their descendants entered the middle class, but then so did the skins of the immigrants who came here late in the twentieth century. In fact those with middle and upper middle class schooling and income were whitened as they set foot in their new country. Caruso was always amazed how rarely his white friends noticed that affluent South Asians were often darker skinned than African Americans.

Poverty seemed to darken immigrant skin colors, however, and the dark skinned poor, South Asians included, were the major targets of racial discrimination and segregation. Consequently, Caruso believed that the faster the nonwhite poor could be helped into the middle class, the more quickly stigmatization, discrimination, and segregation would decline, even if they might never disappear completely. Although legislative and judicial methods of achieving greater racial equality had to continue, greater class equality for racial minorities should slowly erode the racial stereotypes that stigmatized poor nonwhites.

Caruso and later Gordon hoped that the various job and income programs targeted to the below median income population, described in chapter 2, "Healing the Economy," would hasten class equality for the dark skinned poor. In that case, most poor nonwhites could wind up in the economic mainstream before the second half of the century, and the hoary racial stereotypes that marked their ancestors as undeserving would lose the rest of their credibility. Then whites would finally treat them as equals and someday perhaps not even notice their skin colors.

The staffers responsible for making racial policy knew that the process was not quite that simple. For example, some poor people needed only the right parents, some economic and educational resources, and other relevant opportunities to head for the middle class, but others might need a generation in a reasonably secure working class status before they or their children were fully prepared to make it into the middle class. Staying there might take another generation of economic and social security. The pervasive self-confidence found so frequently in the higher classes was probably needed too, but it is mostly a by-product of growing up with affluence.

Moreover, upward mobility takes more than effort by the potentially mobile; the organizations and institutions that patrol the gateways to upward mobility have to cooperate. For example, Caruso pressed hard to restore the affirmative action programs abandoned by the Bush administration or rejected by its courts. His Department of Labor insisted that all agencies and groups receiving public funds must evaluate job applicants by performance or performance-related measures even if they score poorly on tests. Written tests may be quick and cheap, but many people in the below median income population are better performers than test passers.

African Americans

Two populations have been excluded from the whitening process, and both have been in the country longer than whites. One is Native Americans; the other much larger and perhaps even more often excluded one is African Americans. No one is quite sure why they are being kept down longer than other nonwhites. Blackness is hard to whiten, but still whites act more positively toward black West African immigrants. However, American blacks are not immigrants and are distinctive in one respect: they were the country's last slaves, and many were indentured sharecroppers until after World War II.

One would think that because slavery ended in the 1860s, generations born long after would not even resonate to it. However, the first freed slaves, the sharecroppers, and the migrants who became unskilled urban workers and servants were blamed for the economic burdens and other restrictions whites had imposed on them during slavery. Since many of these have been perpetuated generation after generation, poor African Americans are still being blamed for them. In fact, even middle and upper middle class blacks still experience some of the stigmatization and discrimination meted out to poor blacks, as if the dominant classes are out to prevent their upward mobility.

Some observers, black and white, believe that African Americans may be used as pawns in a continuing American search for a permanent bottom class: an "undercaste" that can always be looked down on, disparaged, and kept down so that other populations will feel more worthy. The actual undercaste can be tiny, but its actual size matters little if enough other people need to believe in its pervasiveness. Perhaps the need reflects white shakiness as class and racial inequalities lessen, resulting in the same nativist-like fears still sometimes expressed over the alleged Latinization of white America.

Native Americans are put into somewhat the same undercaste role, especially in the parts of the country in which they are the poorest population. But then whites once viewed them as savages and have made sure that some of their descendants still can be mistreated accordingly.

The Affirmative Reaction

Caruso and Gordon refused to pay attention to such ideas and have continued or revived past antidiscrimination efforts. They have insisted that every taxpayer deserves equal access to public and publicly supported institutions, on class as well as racial grounds. Increased government intervention in economic and other institutions thereby spreads opportunities for equal access.

The Caruso administration began early on to reinterpret the notion of reverse discrimination and, hoping that new terminology would help, called systematically for an affirmative reaction. Administration and other lawyers argued that the centuries-long preferential treatment of whites and the rich justified the preferential treatment of nonwhites and the poor. They claimed further that even quotas were acceptable until a reasonable level of equal representation in public and publicly supported institutions had been achieved.

In addition, they flooded the federal courts with cases, hoping to pressure the Bush-appointed judges who refused to follow the election returns. Then Caruso was able to appoint liberal replacements, and under Gordon, the majority of all federal judges, including on the Supreme Court, are liberals. Although ideology plays only a partial role in the courts, and usually less so among liberals than conservatives, affirmative reaction now stands a far better chance than before.

Racial affirmative reaction has also been complemented by class affirmative action, because now that almost all whites have escaped poverty, the benefits of class affirmative action will go mainly to African Americans and other racial minorities. The civil rights lobbies seek to retain an explicitly racial legal program, however, because nonwhite immigrants are still arriving in the United States. If the courts agree that economic affirmative action can replace its racial predecessors, the Hernandez administration will develop this program further.

In addition, class action suits are now being brought against industries, institutions, and professions that have been the worst offenders in excluding or holding racial minorities back over the last two generations. These suits hark back to the old reparations movement, although redress will be sought only for still living victims.

However, those bringing suit will not ignore the historical past. Lower courts have already affirmed the rights of government or other plaintiffs to seek apologies or at least recognition of guilt from public and private organizations throughout the land that benefited from slavery as well as from the near slavery that Chinese "coolies," the contract laborers imported to build America's railroads, experienced in the nineteenth century.

That cause has been aided as well by the demographic changes that have taken place in the country. The decades of high immigration have spread nonwhite Americans all across the country, so that once totally white parts of the country are now racially diverse. Nearly every American has contact with nonwhites now, and new racial conflict and nativism notwithstanding, prejudice and discrimination have declined.

Ever since the second decade of the twenty-first century, the forces pressing for more racial equality have also been watching intermarriage patterns between whites and nonwhite immigrants, mostly Latin and Asian, hoping that their biracial descendants will affect the racial agenda. Some of the earliest biracials have now married people with other racial mixes and are raising multiracial children. Although multiracial adults are still a small proportion of the electorate, politicians are already wondering with which racial groups and voting blocs they will identify and be identified with. In the longer run, biracials and multiracials may have some interests in common, since many are marginalized by monoracials, white or nonwhite. Perhaps as early as the twenty-second century so many Americans will be multiracial that the remaining monoracial people may cease discriminating against others on the basis of skin color.

The proliferation of multiracials could be hastened, however, by genealogical DNA testing, which suggests that a significant minority of white Americans have African, Caribbean, Latino, Asian, or Native American ancestors. Similarly, many people of one religion will discover they have ancestors of other and not necessarily favored religions. Enough methodological questions have been raised about genealogical testing that many people may choose from the origins that they perceive as most desirable or prestigious. Few are likely to give up racial, ethnic, or religious ancestries that are perceived as superior.

IMMIGRANTS AND THE NATIVE BORN

Ever since the start of the century, traditional race issues sometimes took at least a temporary backseat as native born Americans began to object to the continuing stream of immigrants that had begun about 1965. Although the immigrants, including illegal ones, supplied new vitality to the economy as well as further diversity to the culture and the polity, they had generated another cycle of nativist protests, even if not as violent as those of past centuries.

Part of that protest was clearly racial, because so few of the newcomers were white. Moreover, white native born Americans had been scared by the already mentioned predictions of the country's

Latinization, as well as by the visibility of Spanish speaking people. Many of the scared had forgotten or never knew that they were themselves the descendants of immigrants who had once scared the natives. The below median income community, especially its non-white members, remained fearful that immigrants were taking their jobs or depressing wage levels, or both.

After much money had been spent and antagonisms heightened by unsuccessful attempts to wall off the country, a broad coalition called on the Caruso administration for another round of immigration reform that would strengthen immigration positives and eliminate as many negatives as possible. After his reelection, Caruso set up a commission representing the usual supporters and opponents, its only unusual addition being leaders of senior citizen lobbies and other groups worried about their retirement payments who favored immigration to supply new payees to Social Security.

As the descendant of immigrants, Caruso would have liked the impossible: to admit everyone who wanted to come and to treat all immigrants as equals. Privately, he also favored an immediate pardon for illegal immigrants and wondered if he could obtain enough congressional votes if he concurrently pardoned prominent politicians from both parties then in jail. The commission was made aware of some of his thoughts, and after more than a year of hearings and deliberations, it made its report.

After trying to quiet the fears of anti-immigration forces, the commission recommended dropping both illegality and guest worker statuses as officially condemning immigrants to inferiority and criminalization. In their place, it urged the establishment of a category of probationary immigrants, who could become permanent immigrants in three years and naturalized citizens two years later. The new category would exist alongside the old ones that admitted permanent and temporary immigrants on the basis of various kinds of visas.

Those individuals admitted as probationary immigrants would have the same rights, entitlements, and public services as other immigrants, with one exception: in areas where the living wage was also the minimum wage, employers could hire them for $2 less an hour until they became permanent immigrants; elsewhere it could pay them $1 an hour less.

Probationary immigrants would have to reregister every six months and show that they had found regular although not necessarily full-time employment. Those with families in their country of origin had to show that they were sending remittances to their families; in that case, they could bring spouses and children to the United States once they were certified as permanent immigrants.

Permanent status would usually be awarded to immigrants who had been law abiding. However, all eligible for the higher status and thus likely to be able to make themselves economically useful in their countries of origin would also be offered generous funds to go home to make a new start.

Viewing probationary immigrant status as a substitute for illegal immigration, the commission avoided setting complicated requirements for admission, pointing to those requirements that were already self-selecting illegals: the ability to work hard and long hours as well as good enough health to survive. It suggested the establishment of a dozen or more entrance points modeled to some extent on Ellis Island where those wanting to work in the United States would be admitted or rejected. At least six of the entrance points would be located on the Mexican border; two in Miami; and one each in New York, Chicago, San Francisco, and Los Angeles. The number to be admitted would be determined annually, based on national and regional unemployment rates, estimates of needed workers, and other criteria set by Congress or the White House.

The commission gave entry point officials the right to direct probationary immigrants to, and bar them from, initial moves to specific communities and even states. The probationary immigrants were directed, for example, to agricultural areas needing migrant labor or growing communities seeking construction workers. They were typically barred from communities with high rates of unemployment, particularly among male high school dropouts, with whom immigrants most often competed for jobs, and occasionally from areas where anti-immigrant sentiment was especially intense. Eventually, of course, many would wind up with relatives who had arrived in America earlier, usually in the ever growing number of communities with large immigrant populations.

Probationary immigrants could be deported if they were convicted of crimes or out of work for more than three months, although the jobless and those guilty of property crimes would be offered funds to enable them to make a new start at home in exchange for signing a contract not to return to the United States for five years.

Since almost all immigrants come here to work, the commission further recommended that the Labor Department be given responsibility for administering the program. Labor, it was assumed, would be far less restrictive and punitive than the Immigration and Naturalization Service, which would now be responsible only for visas for permanent immigrants and visitors and passports for citizens.

Although processing probationary immigrants would be costly, the commission believed that illegal immigration attempts would decline sufficiently so that border patrols on land and on sea, as well as the number of policing and judicial agencies currently necessary to control and deport illegals, eventually could be reduced. Expensive attempts to build and rebuild walls could be halted as well.

The commission devoted a whole chapter to the effect of immigration on jobs and wages, especially of unskilled nonwhite American citizens. Its new empirical studies had been as inconclusive as earlier ones, but it argued that jobs labeled as immigrant work were thereby so reduced in status that citizens would take them only as jobs of last resort. The lower wages associated with probationary immigrant status would discourage citizens further. No doubt some citizens lost jobs to immigrants, and other citizens lost wages, although once the living wage became the minimum wage, the wage loss was likely to be minimal.

Caruso had been warned that the commission proposed to eliminate the category of illegal immigrants, and he asked that this proposal be held till after the 2018 election. He hoped that even if Congress rejected the commission's recommendations, at least a new direction for immigration policy was being put forward.

Congress was not pleased with the report, however, and the vocal parts of the general public let Washington know that it would punish all elected officials who voted for unrestricted immigration and against the walls. Probationary immigration was moot and stayed that way during the O'Hara years.

By the time Gordon entered the White House, immigration reform seemed to have a better chance. Latinization fears had died down a little over the last four years as more Latinos Americanized, intermarried, and split their political sympathies and votes in time honored American ways. As increasing numbers of communities and workplaces paid the living wage, more native born workers applied for jobs once taken by immigrants.

Finally Gordon judged that the time was ripe to reintroduce the commission's immigration reform scheme and managed to talk Congress into trying it out for a year, renewable for a second. Angry opponents were promised that the walls on the Mexican border would remain and illegals who broke the law would be deported, but the test would show whether the flow of illegal immigrants could be halted by admitting migrants on a probationary basis. The results would not be known until after Gordon left office, but Hernandez indicated even before he announced for the presidency that he favored all of the commission's proposals.

However, by now, the shortened workweeks that have accompanied economic downturns have also reduced the immigrant flow, at least for the moment. In fact, the drafters of the Community Service Work Program have to decide whether probationary, and even permanent, immigrants will be eligible for the part-time work it will offer.

THE CHANGING GENDER HIERARCHY

The first third of the century has been an ambiguous period for women seeking more gender equality. Gender gaps between women and men have shrunk in all fields, and women have now served both as president and vice president of the United States.

The same egalitarian processes are operating outside government too: where positions are defined by meritorious performance, women are catching up quickly. If present trends continue, top women executives may outnumber men in another generation.

Sharing the housework as well as the responsibility for child care is now expected in most sectors of society when both parents are working. Since Gordon and the Congress have made it easier for parents to take work leave, partners can work out the time with their employers. Sometimes fathers or mothers even decide to stay home longer, choosing the child over the job. Where the wage gap is shrinking, family income considerations no longer play a decisive role in who stays home, and old gender roles are losing their power.

However, women are still set back because *they* have the babies, although sometimes this is only an excuse to preserve male power and turf. Professional and technical employers are reluctant to hire women over men if parenting time reduces either their productivity or their ability to keep up with the latest knowledge. For that reason, women in some professions have their babies when they are young and then move their careers into high gear once the children are in kindergarten. Gordon helped here too: age discrimination that makes it difficult for older women to obtain academic tenure is now prosecuted. In fields like the natural sciences, where original work is often done at the start of careers, women put off having their babies—and do so for longer periods of time as medical advances make ever later childbearing possible. Antidiscrimination laws protect pregnant women, sometimes even against delayed promotions. A handful of firms, mostly owned by or selling to women, give their pregnant workers performance bonuses when the baby arrives.

Glass ceilings that have shattered for women sui generis sometimes disadvantage young mothers, particularly in workplaces in which the highest level jobs require sixty or more hours a week. Such jobs are declining in number, but single or childless women maintain an advantage over mothers that is hard to erase completely.

During the 2020s, many observers believed that as economic and other gender gaps were decreasing, the allegedly genetic or otherwise essentialist gender differences that genetic researchers had posited would disappear. The evidence remains preliminary, but as men spend more time raising children, many seem to become more nurturant, while women executives in highly competitive enterprises have had no trouble winning corporate power struggles. Some women CEOs have sought to cut back unnecessarily competitive relations, especially after observing that this leads to increases in morale and productivity, but the number of so-called alpha females is rising all the time.

Work and home roles are not the same, however, and female alpha executives can be nurturant mothers after work. Role requirements and situational imperatives still shape human behavior, and explanations involving genes become less credible as gender stereotypes weaken. Studies showing that all human beings have traces of maleness and femaleness have been around a long time, but now they are influencing popular constructions of gender.

Gender Politics

Gordon was fearful of losing male voters to the Republicans and therefore shied away from campaigning for the presidency on gender issues. She did state her support for pro choice positions and carefully endorsed abortion, although by now postintercourse pills are making it virtually unnecessary except in cases of rape. She made it a point to nominate women to cabinet and similar top posts in which they had not served previously, for example, Treasury, Defense, and the CIA.

In addition, Gordon initiated a general review of all federal legislation, administrative decisions, guidelines, and the like, to make sure that gender impact was being considered. Thus occupational safety policies and programs have been vetted so that, for example, more attention is being paid to the ergonomic problems of office work, as well as the physical effects on sales and cashier personnel standing eight to ten hours a day. Even the Pentagon is participating, figuring out how to give women more opportunities in special forces units.

Gordon was especially protective of the Democrats' political base in the below median income population and looked for ways to help blue collar mothers deal with the pressures they were under. Although these women had long found it easier than their men to obtain secure jobs, the men remained reluctant to take family burdens off their shoulders. Even if the men helped out more at home than in the past, the women were responsible for the children.

For example, the men continued to be the family's de jure disciplinarians, but the women were still expected to make sure that the children did their homework and were not tempted to join peers who had dropped out of school literally or figuratively.

Gordon looked for ways the federal government could help. She tweaked the recruiting regulations for Caruso's job creation programs to bring working class and poor women into labor markets from which they previously had been excluded. She made sure that women were accepted in the newly created global warming jobs that normally would have gone to men and saw to it that enough women nurses were able to become nurse-doctors.

Later, Gordon was able to include domestic workers in occupations required to pay at least the living wage. She was proudest, however, of quietly intervening in domestic and international scientific circles to obtain a Nobel Prize for a laboratory technician from the Baltimore ghetto who had made a breakthrough in cancer research for which her male supervisor was trying to claim sole credit.

Male Inequality

At the same time, Gordon could brag about taking the first steps in expanding the gender equality agenda to include men. Participating in programs to help below median income mothers, she had learned the extent to which their lives were made more hectic and painful because of their men's difficulties in the labor market. Not only were the women having to work harder and longer hours, but they were at the same time a frequent target for their spouses' frustrations and anger.

The men's plight was not new, but the situation became even more serious over the years as the demand for muscle and other nonprofessional labor continued to decline or the jobs were opened to women. What has not been obvious, at least not in the elite circles inside the Beltway in which presidents are embedded, is that men have been losing out to women in many spheres of life and are now becoming less equal than women.

At all income and educational levels, women are healthier and live longer than men. They are better students than men beginning in elementary school and today receive a majority of academic and professional graduate school degrees. Now that women are catching up in mathematics and the sciences, male dominance is ending in these fields as well.

Better students become abler workers regardless of gender, but perhaps because they have been better students, women are more patient than men in highly competitive situations. Thus, they frequently make more desirable colleagues at the executive level. Patient women are also more productive laboratory scientists, and some labor economists argue that they may be better adapted to the twenty-first-century economy and its constant demand for innovation and negotiation. For this reason, Washington observers suggest, women may make better diplomats than men.

True, observers with their eye on the long range believe that the more women become equal to men, the more they will share shortcomings now correlated with maleness—from increasing rates of heart disease to a readier temptation to resort to verbal and physical violence. Feminists are of course hoping that the women will be able to transform working conditions enough so that even the rate of male heart disease will decline further.

During the years Gordon was in the White House, she could only talk about the apparently changing gender balance. However, the Hernandez administration will have to act. A new approach to gender fairness will be needed: combining programs to reduce remaining areas of female inequality with new programs to help men reverse their declining position in society. This may be the way to achieve gender equality.

The political parties are in a somewhat different quandary. Historically, the Republicans have identified themselves as a party of males ever since white men first left the Democrats in large numbers after the civil rights revolution of the 1960s. Even as they were pursuing the lost men, the Democrats were actively appealing to women, but they also attracted and sought out underdogs. Men are now moving into that category. Both parties are wondering whether women will start voting Republican in greater numbers as they overtake men in the country's pecking orders.

New kinds of gender politics and political conflicts may develop as well. No one is yet talking about male and female voting blocs, but a movement describing itself as masculinist had appeared on the public scene after Gordon's reelection in 2028. It opened an office in Washington and is now recruiting lobbyists with expertise in gender politics.

The movement has raised questions about affirmative action for men, leading some conservative women's groups to make noises about reverse discrimination. Many men agree that they need health care changes to raise male longevity to that of women as soon as possible, and they want a Bureau of Men to complement the Women's Bureau in Washington.

Other male activists are, however, talking and blogging about the need for macho politics and politicians. Experts on downward mobility are worrying whether men for whom the new inequality is particularly traumatic might take out their frustrations on their wives or resort to scapegoating women in general.

Meanwhile, some women leaders are meeting with their peers in the masculinist movement, hoping to use the changing gender hierarchy to encourage a joint push for gender equality. Some think that once enough men experience subordination, they might be more prepared to remove gender as a source of and reason for hierarchy.

SEXUAL EQUALITIES

The pursuit of sexual equality began with the erosion of the double standard for men and women regarding sexual activity before marriage. After the 1960s, that erosion progressed so quickly that government never had a chance to be involved even if it had wanted to. Issues relating to sex were not even on the political agenda.

The double standard has not totally disappeared, but it has been weakened considerably, although men still have other levers for exerting unequal power in sexual relations. Observers of American social change are still surprised at how quickly young women, including adolescents, were freed to participate in premarital sexual activity and at how little political or other protest or punitive legislation followed.

Later, when religious conservatives organized and became extremely active politically to demand state prohibition of abortion and homosexuality and the protection of fetuses, they and other groups sometimes called the anti-sex coalition remained almost totally quiet about teenage sexuality. The coalition limited itself to criticism of the entertainment media and the "permissive" American culture which they blamed for energizing adolescent hormones.

The second phase in sexually equal relations, the decriminalization and acceptance of gay sex, has taken longer and evoked more intense political and other opposition but is now progressing too. Most states outside the major Bible belts have lifted or are ready to lift all prohibitions against consensual sexual relations other than by children.

The straight majority is still uncomfortable with gay sex and even more so with gay marriage, and religous conservatives continue to oppose it. Nonetheless, gays can now marry or live in partnerships virtually as freely as straights and can make their homes almost everywhere, including in mainstream urban and suburban family neighborhoods. Media comics joke that someday gays will be welcome everywhere except in Catholic churches, monasteries, and convents.

The straight majority's accommodation to gays may not be a step in the achievement of sexual equality, but it has taken place. The most common explanation has it that once gay sex was effectively decriminalized and gays could come out of the closet, heterosexual Americans saw that their sexual practices posed no threat to them or, with some notable exceptions, to their children.

Perhaps people realized that the sex lives of gays were the same whether they were married to each other or not and that some straights actually engage in the same sexual practices as gays. In any case, many people seem to have concluded that what couples do in their bedrooms almost never affects the economic, political, and other issues that cause conflict.

Moreover, religious conservatives have discovered that many gay couples are socially and culturally conservative, considerably more in favor of traditional marriage than many straights, and in other respects "squarer" than many heterosexuals. Gay couples also seem to be more affluent than many straights, are unusually good neighbors and defenders of neighborhood property values, recognize their civic duties, and vote Republican surprisingly often. Over time, the number raising children is increasing even as the number of heterosexual parents is still declining.

"Rough trade" as well as transsexualism, S&M, and other sexual fetishisms are still considered deviant practices or diseases, and pedophilia continues to be harshly punished. However, the open practitioners of deviant sex are associated mostly with cities already known to be "sinful." The more flamboyant their deviant behavior, the more they prove that the gays most Americans know as neighbors are as conventional as straights.

As a result, the leaders of the conservative religions are now mulling over what the ministers heading megachurches discovered many years ago: some gays are themselves active and generous church members. The leadership is learning too that even conservative denominations that are losing the younger generation and now accept gay worshippers so that they can survive financially and institutionally usually do so without ill effects on the other church members. And ever since church denials that Jesus was married led to assertions that he was gay, some conservative religious are wondering whether they should stop fighting homosexuality altogether.

A few theologians believe that a more fundamental transformation of the relationship between sex and religion is under way. They point to an early-twenty-first-century novel, *The Da Vinci Code*, which first popularized widely an old scholarly theory that Jesus was married—and to Mary Magdalene, with whom he was raising children. The novel is said to have attracted more than forty million readers when it was first published, although no one knows how much it expressed popular support for the view of Jesus as a spouse.

If so many people were ready to entertain the notion that Jesus was a conventional heterosexual, they might also be ready to believe that Christianity had no reason to judge sexual behavior and punish some sexual practices. If Jesus and his wife practiced birth control as well, the theological opposition to abortion might have to be rethought. Undoubtedly, the easy availability of birth prevention medicine has made a difference too, as has the recent assertion by some newly founded religions that religions might lack all justification for regulating sexual behavior.

The politicians are watching these developments quietly. Although the journalists pressed Hernandez to comment during the 2032 campaign, he steadfastly refused, in order, he said, to uphold the separation of church and state. Privately, he is relieved that one possibly incandescent issue is off his table.

RELIGIOUS EQUALITY AND THE RISE OF THE SECULARS

The White House is staying on the sidelines about another issue; the general decline of religion as a cultural and political force. Not only have many religious conservatives retreated from politics, but the mainline religions are still losing members and worshippers. A large number of the remaining worshippers are moving toward the now widespread high holiday pattern; coming only for the most important religious holidays, Christmas, Easter, and the Jewish High Holidays particularly.

Some of the nonattenders celebrate at home, sharing meals and presents and raising the possibility that the mainline religions may eventually turn into dinner religions for adults and presents religions for children, with the holidays designed for children likely to survive the longest. Early versions of these trends are now being seen even among Muslim and other minority religions and even among the most conservative Christians and Jews.

However, the most dramatic change has been the literal coming out of the seculars: people who say they do not believe in a god and do not gather to pray or socialize in churches or other places of worship. Quietly secular Americans may have been around longer and in larger numbers than anyone imagined, but since the pollsters were not curious about them, they were not visible. Once they came out, established Web sites to explain themselves, and created opportunities for blogging and other Internet interactions, the number of interested people grew rapidly. Evidently many people had either been hiding or waiting to share their feelings and ideas.

Since seculars do not proselytize or seek converts, they are only minimally organized. All they really have in common is their rejection of gods and of what they call the theistic sacred—the spheres of life that are dominated or influenced by religion. Still, they do not deny the notion of sanctity, and they insist that the social, cultural, political, and other values that they defend are sacred to them.

Although the media like to pit seculars against atheists and agnostics for Sunday morning media discussions, most seculars lack interest in disproving or even debating the existence of gods. For them, deities are cultural creations or social constructions that still exist only because many humans need them and therefore created them. Not feeling that need, seculars live without deities.

Even so, seculars defend the right of people to create gods for themselves, and they favor tolerance of all religions that are themselves tolerant of other religions. They admit that religions and gods are suppliers of assurance, therapy, and peace of mind. When they cannot find other help, seculars admit that they too sometimes turn to prayer.

Seculars are indifferent to religious politics, at least until issues such as the church-state separation, religious tax exemptions, and religious justifications for war and other forms of violence come up. They support the first and oppose the rest but realize that they are currently a minority and that their views will probably not be taken into account.

As a result, the initial secular spokespersons and leaders, most self-selected, do not know if they can mobilize their fellow seculars or establish a citizen lobby. They are not even sure that they want to, for they are not eager to give the conservative and mainline religions a reason to organize against them. And without houses of worship or other forms of real estate, seculars lack the material interests that help to spur active religious involvement in politics.

At the moment, seculars are actually mainly concerned with what they consider their distinctive spiritual issue: to demonstrate that a godless universe does not deprive human existence and human life of meaning. Instead, they argue—along lines familiar to philosophers but not yet to the general American public—that even if the purposes and meanings of life do not originate with gods, they are not random or arbitrary. People make their own meanings, and thus they must decide, as individuals and groups, what purposes they see in life, what goals they want to achieve, what values they will advocate, and what choices they will make when they must choose.

Seculars are aware that gods are social control and conformity mechanisms that make sure that most people act in accepted ways whether through willed or enforced obedience. Secularism aims neither for social control nor for conformity, and the disappearance of gods from the public sphere will probably intensify public disagreements about purposes, goals, values, and choices.

Nonetheless, seculars are confident that in the long run, people will be readier to agree or to compromise about purposes, goals, values, and choices once the obstacle of religion is removed. They are, however, also hopeful that democratically elected governments and other institutions can make room for discussions of these issues. But they are realistic about how long this could take.

Moreover, seculars are not of one mind on what they call the meaning of life question or on concrete everyday issues. Democratic seculars do not often agree with Republican seculars, nor do secular entrepreneurs concur with welfare state supporters. Secular landlords fight with secular tenants, and creators of high culture look down on their popular culture peers even if they see eye to eye on secularism. Seculars can be just as determined and combative as anyone else when they are defending their economic, cultural, and other values and interests.

Before he decided to stand for the presidency, Hernandez identified himself as a secular but treated it as a private and personal matter unrelated to his political activities and beliefs. Needless to say, he received flak from the Latino part of his base that was also Catholic or Protestant. He received even more flak from Latino religious leaders, especially when these found out that many in their flocks would vote for a godless Hernandez as enthusiastically as for a believing one.

Hernandez never campaigned as a secular, but he freely answered the many questions he received from journalists and prospective voters. Although he never mentioned gods in his campaign speeches, he visited the worship services of every major religion and denomination on the campaign trail that would have him and talked with all of the country's religious heads.

So far in Hernandez's presidency, no secular issues or issues that conflict with his beliefs have surfaced, although like any other president, he has met with religious leaders from all over the world. Perhaps no such issues will come up while he is in the White House, but sometimes he is said to wonder whether it might be politically possible to ask Congress to reduce or eliminate religious tax exemptions and deductions before he leaves the Oval Office.

CHAPTER FIVE

FAMILY, HOME, AND COMMUNITY

When Caruso was running for the presidency, *family values* was still a potent campaign term, signifying opposition to abortion; gay marriage; and, in some parts of the electorate, even birth control. He used one of his campaign speeches to suggest that these had more to do with sex and procreation than the family, but the reaction was vocal and negative, persuading him to say no more about family values even after he was in the White House.

Subsequently, Caruso added that he even preferred to do without an explicit family policy. Since nearly everyone lived in or was connected to some kind of family or household, the government would do all it could, and would push private enterprise to do all it could, to help families and households achieve their values.

However, government, at least, would stop at the borders of people's private worlds and would not intrude into the intimate and other relations that constitute family life. The Caruso administration, and, Caruso hoped, all future ones, would intervene mainly to help victims of demonstrable pathological forces in the society and protect them and other vulnerable people from victimizers and victimizing social forces.

Caruso's use of the term *demonstrable* was his way of sending a message to the family values advocates who imagined pathologies that do not exist or that exist only in connection with moral codes that no longer have much public support. As noted in the last chapter, birth control technology is virtually eliminating the need for abortion and the opposition to it, and same sex unions are on the way to becoming mainstream.

Marriage itself may one day take on less importance because partners, heterosexual or homosexual, are acquiring the same legal rights as spouses. Discussion of sex is now being framed in the language of tolerance instead of morality, and a few political and religious leaders already talk about majority and minority sexualities and praise sexual diversity.

THE NUCLEAR FAMILY

In 2017, when Vice President Grant started thinking about succeeding Caruso in the White House and about policies she would highlight in her campaign, the family allowance was high on her list. Not coincidentally, she and Caruso brought up the nuclear family during one of their weekend TV discussions. They mentioned it only in passing, but it evoked an unusual number of e-mails from parents and older adults.

After a White House poll indicated that many people were still concerned about the decline of the nuclear family, a few more discussions of the subject were scheduled. Then the White House assembled some of the administration's family experts, who tried to reassure people that nuclear families were as significant as ever but that they no longer consisted solely of two spouses or partners and children.

Now, the actual child rearing might be done by a duet, one of whom was a stepparent or a grandparent; by two unmarried partners; by a single parent; or by some other combination of individuals. Sometimes, especially in immigrant families, the oldest daughter was a major participant in raising the younger children—a centuries old practice that somehow had been omitted from public descriptions of parenting. Moreover, the child rearing family was now often embedded in larger households, which could include one or more other families from several generations, siblings, other relatives, in-laws, and even coparenting former spouses or partners. Finally, housekeepers, nannies, babysitters, day care workers, and school-teachers were added to the list.

Although the discussions accurately described reality in the second decade of the century, conversation on the topic of the family allowance revived the defenders of the traditional nuclear family that had dominated much of twentieth-century American life and even more of its discourse. Before long, enough debates over the nuclear family, some very bitter, had erupted from all points on the ideological spectrum that the vice president quietly buried her idea of a family allowance.

In Caruso's political travels, he, like his successors, had come across even more diversity: people who lived together in relationships so distinctive that they would not have made believable soap opera plots. Caruso was especially taken with some polygamous households he had encountered in the Northeast. They seemed happy with their arrangement, which was particularly suitable for communities in which women outnumbered men. They could normally cope with occasional bouts of jealousy, including among the many children, and were sad only that they could not marry, for then they would be breaking the law.

Like other Americans, the occupants of the Oval Office sometimes wished that family life was simpler, but that was not going to happen. Like the country, the family was changing, but only among the very poor was it breaking apart in dangerous numbers. Actually, family values were not even in danger and had not changed as much as families themselves. The real problem was that sometimes people could not put their values into practice.

Family Policies

Consequently, all of the presidents, including O'Hara, pursued what are now called family cohesion policies: new ways to help child rearing units, whether they were traditional nuclear families or not, to stay together. For example, Caruso, who liked to talk about the centrifugal forces that pulled families apart, called for moving allowances to enable workers taking new low and moderate wage jobs in other parts of the country to bring their spouses and children.

Feeling that she needed to offset being single, Gordon made families, households, and family policies a major theme in her presidential campaign. But by the time she won the election, she realized that the theme also sometimes made her feel motherly, which, as it turned out, also raised her approval rating.

Gordon began by appointing a special assistant for family to the White House staff who advocated a general family allowance, but she soon decided that such a policy made little sense given the country's familial diversity, and she opted for specific family policies. For example, Gordon sought help for single parent families or households, believing that one person should not have to bear the child rearing burden alone. As noted in the last chapter, she sought to create the economic conditions enabling single mothers to marry. However, Gordon also persuaded Congress that the government should offer modest financial and other aid to assure the presence of a second parent to others, although that parent could be anyone: a lover, a sibling, a grandparent, or a fictive family member. The same aid was extended to isolated families who lacked a supportive family network or were without nearby relatives, especially in times of crisis.

Years earlier, Caruso had gotten credit for family building legislation that provided parental work leaves for family crises. Defining fundable crises took some time, because the leaves were paid for by a subsidized family crisis insurance program that was at the same time another payoff to the health insurance companies for their losses following the creation of the single payer medical plan.

The Gordon administration moved beyond the leaves program by resurrecting an old twentieth-century scheme for job sharing, which encouraged two workers to share a single job. Originally intended for people who wanted to work part-time, for example, during their child rearing days, job sharing was revamped to allow couples with similar skills to divide up one full-time job. The scarcity of eligible sharers and a myriad of logistical problems mean the program will always be small, and it may become unworkable if and when the full-time workweek declines further, although then the sharers can be accommodated by the Community Service Work Program.

Gordon's singlehood gave rise to one more White House concern: the rising number of childless families and households. Despite the fact that some singles eventually bear or adopt children, more couples and most of the men and women who remain single have been opting for voluntary childlessness, wanting to devote their time to other pursuits, particularly self-exploration and development, in which children can easily get in the way.

Gordon's concern was hardly new. Critics had long been condemning the individualism that underlies childlessness, as well as the disappearance of the obligation to perpetuate society and the human species. And others decried the immigrants' role in replenishing the country's supply of children.

Whether many ever felt obliged to perpetuate the human species can be doubted, but the traditional needs for children are shrinking. Children's ability to work, bring in a dowry, and assist the family's upward mobility and dynasty building are no longer required. Children still offer satisfaction and pleasure as love objects, as contributors to family cohesion, and as the fulfillment of people's desire to reproduce themselves, particularly by women, but they are no longer universally thought to be essential.

Gordon was too practical a politician to tell childless voters to multiply, but she knew from personal experience that people sometimes changed their minds about children as they became older. Consequently, she set some wheels in motion to speed up adoption reform, in Washington and at the United Nations, making it easier for healthy but older people to adopt orphaned children.

Social Counselors and Demon Chasers

A common theme ran through the White House ventures into family policy: to make family life less problematic and more comfortable. Having lived among social workers, Caruso was sensitive to the virtues and shortcomings of counseling. As a result, he wanted to see how it could be coordinated with the administration's economic and other policies to alleviate the problems that led people to seek the help of counselors.

What Caruso called social counseling has not yet materialized, but indirectly it led to two programs that have now become Beltway buzzwords. One is the 811 phone line, an emergency hotline for people with family and household problems and conflicts. Although callers employ a very loose definition of both, the line has offered emergency help and some support to temporarily or regularly troubled families.

The second program is demon chasing, which began when Gordon asked her cabinet one day whether the government had ever thought to help people rid themselves of the demons that caused them continuing anxiety and led to conflicts with family, friends, and workmates. The media had a field day with the idea, but focus groups indicated public support, and Gordon assembled a team to explore a demon-chasing program. Gordon was wise enough to make no promises, and now the Hernandez administration must decide whether to initiate the program.

Still, the possibility of offering the voters an emotionally more comfortable life is intriguing, and Democratic party strategists are eager to make that offer. However, the White House is well aware that untroubled people require an untroubled society, which it cannot now produce.

YOUNG PEOPLE AND OLD PEOPLE

In addition to starting family programs, Caruso and his successors have initiated life cycle programs for adolescents and the old—the two major life cycle groups outside the conventional labor market. Hernandez initiated the young people's program when he served as Caruso's Secretary of Education, but, having been a junior high teacher, he urged redefining the program's boundaries. Adolescence is a category created by adults, and as young people obtain more responsibilities, the category itself could change. Even now, seventeen-year-olds rarely associate with fifteen-year-olds, although adults classify them both as teenagers.

Adults also set the boundaries between childhood and adolescence, but thanks to the earlier onset of puberty and to full access to much of the adult world, especially through the digital media, childhood is being cut back and adolescence advanced—and lengthened.

In some respects, adolescence is even merging with young adulthood, as full adulthood is put off. For the educated middle class, but not for it alone, reasonably secure jobs and careers, as well as marriage and parenthood, come later than in the past.

The Merging of Adolescence and Young Adulthood

Soon after Hernandez was appointed Caruso's Secretary of Education, he obtained control over all of the federal government's activities involving adolescents. However, because he knew that teenagers were reluctant to endorse programs determined for them by adults, many of his beginning ideas originated with Beltway adolescents, including his own adolescent niece and nephew and the children of other Hernandez administration staffers.

Acting informally, the Beltway youngsters used various adolescent messaging platforms for programmatic suggestions. Then they pressed Hernandez and his staff to establish a temporary national office in which they could brainstorm issues that might benefit from national help.

The youngsters' first idea was overly ambitious and so far has been unsuccessful: designing a school social structure that would reduce teenage peer pressure, as well as bullying and harassment of vulnerable students. This proposal is always revived whenever school shootings, student suicides, violence at athletic events, and other disruptions of the school social order take place.

In addition, the adolescent brainstormers wanted more accountability from and influence over the school personnel that controlled them. They asked for the right to vote no confidence in, or petition for recalls of, school personnel they considered oppressive, and they wanted to organize referenda about needed or unwanted school practices. Many school boards, administrators, teachers, and parents were horrified, but eventually Hernandez established a variety of accountability procedures that satisfied the students.

The young people also advocated helping students begin to develop or at least think about their occupational interests as they moved through high school. The teenagers agreed that they should not make career decisions while still in school, but they proposed—and Hernandez quickly endorsed—an early internship program that would inform interested students, especially those unlikely to go to college, about a variety of occupations and careers available to them.

The internships would begin during summer vacations for four-teen-year-olds but later could be turned into half year or yearlong part-time jobs. The former would be unpaid; the latter would pay at least the teenage minimum wage, but Congress added special bonuses for students who were contributing to the family income or needed to work to make money for college. Employers who wanted to hold on to their interns could even pay for their college educations and hire them for full-time jobs.

The idea generated only scattered opposition from employers who needed young people for unskilled jobs and from colleges worrying about the future of their interning programs. The high schools mostly worried that the internship program could ruin extracurricular school activities, but as might have been expected, the best interns also found the most time for such activities.

Critics point out that internships have become a new occupational stratum, with even paying internships offering wages below the federal minimum. The classical Left sees them as a new form of capitalistic exploitation; the modern Left believes they should be unionized. The Gordon administration agreed to support the idea of unions. Although Congress mandated that no one could be fired to make room for interns, the unions are still worried that in the long run interns will mean fewer jobs for full-time and adult workers.

The young people have welcomed the opportunity to try different jobs, and career counselors, stymied by generations of young people who did not know what to do with their lives, are happy that these possibilities are available. The internship program could even bring about some of the changes that the adolescents have sought for the school social structure. As interning students develop new interests, they might pay less attention to the school social structure, and its importance, as well as the effects of peer pressure, might diminish.

The Old and Once Old

The boundary changes at the end of the life cycle have been more complicated than those at the start. With the number of fully active people in their eighties and nineties increasing and centenarians no longer being newsworthy, health has replaced chronology as a measure of age. Thus, healthy seventy-year-olds are now described as being in their senior middle age, old age currently beginning at eighty. As always, the counting is partly political, for many baby boomers had turned eighty by the time that Hernandez took office.

The changes in old age and senior citizenship designation have policy implications galore. People who spent their lives at muscle labor and other repetitive and servile jobs still try to retire early if they can afford to, but a number of healthy eighty-year-olds want to work, and some of those who have retired want to unretire.

Yet another set of older people, many of them professionals, would like to give up their regular duties but remain a part of the organizations in which they spent much of their working lives. Borrowing an idea floated by the sociologist Arlie Hochschild, they suggest that such people move into an unpaid but permanent sabbatical status inside the workplace organization. They would be free to work whenever they wanted to, and they would avoid or at least lessen the marginal or useless feelings that accompany retirement. If such a status is organizationally feasible, careers need no longer end with retirement. Some gerontologists would even ban or at least replace the word *retirement.*

Government's problem is that in an economy with recurring job scarcities, older people who want to work will be depriving younger people of work. Since the old vote more often than young people and senior lobbies support their demands, the White House is trying to find a way out. One suggestion is to increase Social Security payments for senior middle aged and senior workers who give up their jobs to younger people. Another is to use tax incentives to encourage them to undertake volunteer work instead.

However, the administration is also looking for novel work programs that do not require large federal outlays. The Library of Congress had asked Gordon to inaugurate a life history program, which encourages and subsidizes seniors nominally to write memoirs or even full autobiographies. So far, only a small number have produced memoirs, however. If money can be found, interviewers will be hired to collect oral histories, especially from people known to have participated in or observed historically significant events earlier in their lives.

In addition, Gordon's Department of Labor tried to help retired people with locally marketable skills to start small businesses in fields such as repair, specialty cooking, collectibles trading, and the like. In some places, the seniors provided heretofore unavailable services, but in others they competed with a lively but virtually invisible array of off-the-books and barter enterprises.

Now Hernandez's Department of Labor will identify seniors with historically and otherwise useful but no longer marketable skills and help them find customers, for example, people who can teach obsolete computer languages and word processing programs and those who can repair manual typewriters and other mass produced goods from the last century. Museums are particularly eager for and will help fund such workers.

Terminal Pain Relief

To no one's surprise, health policy remains a major concern for seniors. Despite early fears that the health expenditures required by an aging population could bankrupt the country, the opposite is happening. As more people are living longer without disabling illnesses, an ever larger number can be served by the nurse-doctor program (see chap. 2, "Healing the Economy") before they face diseases that require calling in specialists. However, because some previously terminal diseases are becoming curable, many who now die at a later age do so in their sleep, the most painless form of death for them as well as the national treasury.

Still, painful chronic illness is also on the increase, and as more and more people reach their eighties and nineties, many of the painfully ill among them now feel entitled to pain relief. A variety of alternative painkillers, including medical marijuana, are now legal all over the country. In some states, very sick old people who want to enjoy their remaining time on Earth can now obtain mind-expanding drugs, including even LSD. The notion that death can be pleasurable disturbs those who believe that the drug takers might be on their way to hell, but their cultural influence is waning.

The positive reception to the idea of a pleasurable death revived an old social movement which demanded that terminally ill people facing a painful end be given the right to die. This movement quickly teamed up with the hospices that administer pain relief to the terminally ill, as well as a group of medical doctors and nurse-doctors who reject the notion that the health profession has to prolong even the most unbearable lives.

Needless to say, the doctors in favor of helping to end unbearable lives aroused the opposition of the mainstream medical profession. However, the new breed of medics is now obtaining the support of several senior citizen lobbies. These doctors are also hoping to grow enough to organize as an independent profession. Then they will be able to separate themselves sufficiently from the mainstream medical profession, both to protect themselves and to spare the latter the conflict between eliminating suffering and prolonging life. Once independent they will also have to take on the religions who still oppose suicide in any form and for any reason.

True, the moral and other issues that accompany assisted suicide remain. Nonetheless, the medical technologies, pain killers, home remedies, and even third world medicines that can end lives are so numerous now that desired deaths are hard to stop.

HOME POLICIES

For Caruso, home was the place for family life, and he managed to talk his Secretary of Housing into distinguishing home policy from housing policy. Home policy seeks to make sure that people get the home they want and can afford, and in fact, its prime mission is to make sure that renters and buyers can obtain and hold onto housing affordable for them. Even so, those who make home policy also aim to help architects, builders, and government fit future new and rebuilt dwelling units to the needs of families and households. As a result, home policy officials can now be found in federal agencies involved in family policy, working alongside, if not always peacefully, the traditional developers and analysts of housing policy known as "housers."

Even as home policy is finding its place, it is being transformed by a changing world. Although originally created to take account of the transformations in family and household structure, it also had to adapt to the work and income uncertainties of homeowners and tenants and continuing high housing prices and rents.

Then, the rising cost of energy, global warming policy, and the demand for "green development" have further complicated the home policy mandate—and its housing implications. For example, the green developers have created two- and three-family houses that can share climate and plumbing systems. Some new low density communities are experimenting with three-family compounds: three houses built on two lots but around a common utility core. Most of the multifamilial housing is suitable for several branches or generations of the same family, but sometimes three or more families who are friends try to live together. Family conflicts can often be neutralized with a little extra soundproofing.

"Mother-daughter" houses, granny flats, semidetached row houses, and other existing units were already available in most large communities. Many of the oversized McMansions put up since the later years of the twentieth century could be rebuilt into multifamily housing.

House and apartment design have been affected as well. Group and even community heating and cooling systems are being tried in much new housing construction. In all but the harshest climates, some people are leaving rooms unheated in winter or uncooled in summer. Houses that can be partially closed off for this purpose have become more popular.

High energy costs are also responsible for the disappearance of the living room. Having taken second place to the family room for decades, it is often either completely eliminated in new construction or, more often, relegated to a formal corner of the family room. Luxury housing is now defined in part by the retention of the living room. Decorative fireplaces and cathedral ceilings have become virtually extinct. In very cold and very warm climates, houses sometimes come with only a front door to reduce the loss of heated and cooled air—and with a higher bill for fire insurance.

Most people who can afford to do so still choose their neighborhoods by traditional criteria: proximity to family, friends, work, and the like. However, some want to live with others of the same family type, and as a result, several Secretaries of Housing have encouraged some building and planning experiments.

The most challenging experiments were undertaken to fit the lifestyles of the many different kinds of people long called singles, those preferring to live alone and those wanting or needing to share residences. Their increasing number has encouraged the reinvention or modernization of the rooming house and apartment hotel of the distant past, including some built to fit the special needs of older singles.

Experimental singles neighborhoods, mostly in the suburbs, revived the inclusion of public dining rooms and private as well as public meeting places, some modeled on plans used earlier in housing for the elderly. Some singles areas included single parents, particularly middle class ones who depend on reciprocal help arrangements with other single parents, but they also wanted single men nearby, some for protection, others for relationships. In other experiments, singles, childless couples, and older people could choose to be together in child-free areas, although it turned out that even the voluntarily childless liked having a few children nearby. Not all singles wanted to live with other singles either, and some family dominated communities used zoning to keep out singles areas.

Some experimental neighborhoods flourished and have subsequently become more widely available. Others did not survive because people preferred neighborhood diversity to demographic compatibility, especially when diversity included the freedom to keep neighborhood relations friendly but distant.

Architects, builders, and planners learned a lot about the attractions and downsides of diversity and homogeneity, including when and for whom age homogeneity remained important and who was willing and able to tolerate diversity in class, status, and race. In fact, everyone who was involved in these experiments, including politicians, later admitted that they learned a great deal—above all that it is a poor idea to use physical design to enforce social mixing of strangers.

The homes policy has begun to change housing design, the many experimental projects having encouraging architects and builders to consult the eventual owners or first tenants or bring them into the design process. Sometimes families or households are encouraged to begin the process of designing new or rebuilt houses and apartments. Group design meetings with eventual occupants of multifamilial and singles housing have also been employed, after which the future occupants were sent home with computer software to try other layouts. These innovations have increased costs, and some may not survive an economic downturn.

However, the raised design expectations have already impacted architecture and planning. Architectural theorists are talking about user-oriented design and about designing from the inside out. For well over a decade, the profession's hottest buzzword has been bottom up or BU architecture, which begins with talking at length to eventual occupants or people like them and even having them undertake draft designs.

Architectural education has undergone a revolution. For instance, students of BU architecture, supervised by designers with sociological training, spend their first year observing housing and workplace uses in cities and suburbs and study the designs chosen by middle and lower income people who have built their own homes.

Architectural critics are not happy with the new design theories, partly because user-oriented and BU design reflect popular taste, ignore professional aesthetic guidelines, and eschew philosophical commentary on the state of contemporary society. Some critics fear that their power and even their usefulness are declining but others are inventing a new architectural criticism, based on studies of how well user-oriented and BU designs satisfy the needs and wishes of the occupants.

SOCIAL HOUSING

Caruso was already a homeowner when housing prices began to climb in the late twentieth century, and he was an elected official when the housing bubble burst and home prices tumbled. Thus he never forgot his father's frequently repeated plaint that housing ought to be a utility, just like "the gas and electric." Caruso shared his belief, but when running for president, he said only that families in the below median income population should not have to pay more than 25 percent of their income for decent housing. He also proposed that homeowners in the below median income population who were financially in over their heads should be able to rent their homes until they had recovered financially enough to resume mortgage payments or were able to find cheaper housing.

In addition, a national community organization obtained foundation money to buy some foreclosed homes in the hardest hit parts of the country and make the homes available to other foreclosure victims on a rental or lease-purchase basis. The scheme became sufficiently successful to expand it to other areas of the country, and later, Gordon incorporated it into a larger federal program that might someday do away with foreclosures altogether.

Initially, Caruso hoped that he could raise incomes sufficiently for everyone to pay for decent and large enough housing in a desired location. He had also hoped to initiate a major wave of housing construction as part of his job creation offensive, but residential building was no longer as labor intensive as it had been in the twentieth century. Finding inexpensive land on which to build in areas of the country where housing was most needed was also more difficult than in the past.

To get the housing program off to a quick start, Caruso persuaded Congress to revive a twentieth-century idea: insured below market loans for all war veterans in the below median income population. Later, the Pentagon offered the same deal as a recruitment bonus to all enlisted personnel with families.

To attract investors and builders, the Caruso administration briefly offered a cost plus construction financing grant, an old wartime scheme that Caruso thought could sometimes be diverted to peacetime uses. The plus was set to guarantee the builder a 6 percent profit, but local communities could ask for a higher profit where affordable housing was more badly needed. Unfortunately, the housing program is so expensive that it has to be cut back in hard times, just when economic theory suggests its expansion.

Finally, just before he left office, Caruso got Congress to revitalize the old Hope VI program that built mixed income projects on land where public housing projects once stood. However, he asked Congress to call it just Hope and guarantee that no low income residents would be permanently displaced. Congress also authorized such projects to be built on other publicly owned sites, including post offices emptied by e-mailing and government back offices emptied essentially by software.

Private or NGO builders would erect the houses and apartment buildings; the government would act as developer only if no one else was willing. The program would also include rehabilitated units. Everything had to be built by union labor, but builders could construct modular unit housing as long as it was built by unionized factory labor. In return, the White House leaned hard on the construction unions to revoke unreasonable building rules.

O'Hara tabled the scheme before it could get started, but Gordon revived it after her election. Her housing team gave the name "social housing" to the homes created by the new program, borrowing a now forgotten twentieth-century European term to indicate that the homes were available to anyone willing to pay the rent. The new name would also distinguish—and distance—this housing from existing public housing even though most of the units were intended for the below median income population, including the poor.

In communities where vacant land was in short supply, builders were encouraged to build infill housing, preferably wherever at least three and no more than ten adjacent and nearly adjacent vacant residential building lots were available. Thus some mass production building techniques could be employed.

Where vacant or eligible public land was not available and local building and zoning codes could be revised, federal and local governments enabled local builders and housing agencies to obtain houses and apartment buildings that could be rehabilitated or rebuilt at slightly higher densities, thus adding as many units as possible to the supply of social housing. Later, a court decision that enabled communities to use eminent domain to increase the supply of housing affordable to the poor provided an unexpected spur to the social housing program.

Integrating Social Housing

At the end of the 2020s, social housing was off and running, but while it attracted some lower middle and even a few upper middle class residents, the affluent stayed away. A number of communities wanted to build more luxurious residences for the affluent to supply the less well off residents with role models to inspire their escape from poverty. However, the poor indicated that they needed no role models, and most of the well-to-do residents had come as graduate students and young professionals who stayed on even though they could have moved to more prestigious areas.

Calling the new housing social has not made tenants with different incomes eager to live together. The better off among them depend on their homes or neighborhoods to announce their social status; the poor cannot afford to keep up with nonpoor Joneses—or even to buy their children the toys with which the Jones children play. As a result, poor and nonpoor residents need some isolation from each other. Often the availability of a slightly wider street or a small park enables better off residents to create a symbolic boundary that serves their status needs without making the poor feel subjected to extra stigma. Nor does such a boundary discourage those ready to transcend economic differences.

The Hernandez housers are already involved in a bitter policy debate. Some want to make further attempts to increase the proportion of middle class occupants; others want to maximize the amount of housing available to the poor.

Some housers would also like to resume building public housing for poor people who want to live together and away from disapproving "betters." The advocates of this policy would like to demonstrate that the problems public housing encountered and the negative reputation it earned in the twentieth century resulted from the Republicans' withdrawal of maintenance funds for the housing and income supports for its very poor residents. Although they admit that public housing concentrates poverty, they can also show that with a little economic help and a lot more respect, fewer residents escape into drugs and drug dealers can be kept out of the projects. Some public housing supporters emphasize the dangers of concentrating the rich.

Social housing is racially more integrated than other new housing, perhaps because it attracts a slightly more liberal set of renters, particularly in the South. People similar in class are apparently readier to live interracially with every new generation, but the easiest way to overcome white objections to racial integration is to attract biracial and multiracial families.

Racial integration is also facilitated because all social units are rentals. When people do not need to worry about their property values, minorities of any kind are less threatening.

Housing the Very Poor

In some communities, even the poor complained about overly permissive mixing. The strivers wanted to keep their distance from those who lacked the strength and opportunities to escape poverty, and no one wanted to be near the very poorest people, as well as the troubled people, poor or not, including those who made trouble for their neighbors as well as themselves.

Some of the troubled poor were willing and able to move to the handful of supported social housing units available. There they received professional help in addition to shelter. However, most of the troubled poor eventually wind up in the poorest or most deserted parts of their communities and often at the very edges of metropolitan areas. Hernandez now wants to require, and help, local governments to provide them the services associated with supported housing. Difficult as some poor people are, they do pay taxes and deserve to be treated as members of the community. Moreover, their children will be offered opportunities to escape the troubled life short of separating them from their parents.

COMMUNITY PLANNING, ENERGY COSTS, AND GLOBAL WARMING

Even while the Caruso and Gordon administrations were participating in housing policy innovations, they also had to think of how community and housing policy questions related to car use, energy cost, and global warming issues.

The Caruso administration, and the Gordon administration subsequently, began with the assumption that although Americans would not soon give up their cars, the higher cost of gasoline and its substitutes was forcing most to drive ever smaller cars, at least for regular commutes in the denser parts of the country. Federal weight taxes added extra pressure, but in order to cut back on the use of oil and to reduce carbon dioxide emissions, speed limits were also reduced in most of the country. This process was described in chapter 3, "Moving toward World Peace and Planetary Survival."

Still, the two administrations and their long-range planners also sought to discourage future car use by expanding and adding to the existing mass transit systems and making them viable substitutes for the car. For this purpose the administrations had to consider three issues.

One issue was whether and how a significant proportion of the people who expected to live in single family homes could be persuaded to accept higher density housing and eventually even apartment living. A second was whether mass transit should be available to all but the smallest and most isolated communities. The third issue might have been the most daunting: whether this continent-sized country would someday have to move closer together and desert some of its virtually empty and emptying areas so as to save energy.

All three issues create the usual policy and political problems associated with long-range planning, but they are also overlaid with countervailing considerations that haunt those responsible for them: what if new oil deposits are found that drastically reduce the price of fuel at the pump, a long lasting and inexpensive car battery is perfected, and global warming trends are suddenly halted and even reversed. Long-range planning could perhaps continue "on paper," but Congress is likely to stop appropriating money for permanent and costly changes the moment current threats disappear.

Raising the National Density

Raising the national density is an old issue, and the moment it appeared on the federal agenda, professional and amateur urbanists revived century-old arguments advocating the elimination of "sprawl." They propose a gradual emptying out of low density areas in favor of old and newly built high density communities. Privately, urbanists speak of getting Americans out of their single family houses, but no one is ready to put it so baldly in public.

The past opponents of sprawl did not have to consider fuel shortages and global warming, but, preaching urbanism with an almost religious fervor, they did not even think very hard about the effect of density increases on land values and housing prices. They did not investigate how the costs of the massive rehousing would be paid: for example, they did not consider the fact that suburban homeowners, unable to sell their now valueless houses, would not be able to convert equity into down payments on the new high density housing. Nor did the urbanists consider that the land values of present and future high density areas would skyrocket. The resulting gentrification would force most of the remaining below median income urban residents out of the cities and the higher density suburbs. Many would probably wind up in the low density areas that were being emptied, thereby reinventing sprawl.

The White House always paid its respects to the influential professionals and citizens lined up against sprawl, but the politicians were well aware that most homeowners and many aspiring ones wanted to live at the lowest densities they could—or even could not—afford. In the twentieth century, young couples, at least in the above median income population, bought their first single family house before the arrival of the second child. By the turn of the century the first house was apt to be a row house or a townhouse, although eventually, families still expected to wind up in a single family home. That, in any case, is the current American dream, even though an ever larger proportion of families can no longer achieve it.

To be sure, many prospective homeowners had already resigned themselves to a slow but continuing rise in overall density. However, they would try very hard to avoid spending their adult lives in apartments. In pursuit of the American dream of homeownership, they would rethink their family budgets, take extra jobs, and spend their retirement funds. In the process, they would probably vote any government out of office that seriously questioned their American housing dream. Many might even decide that global warming would never become serious enough to give up the dream.

Caruso's early statements on raising America's density were so restrained as to be out of character for him. He emphasized that although overall residential, commercial, and other densities would have to rise, no one would be forced to move to cities. He also promised to prevent American versions of twenty-first-century state of the art Asian cities, many of which are solidly built up with sixty-story skyscraper apartment houses.

Instead, the Caruso administration began a national conversation about density, using the Caruso-Grant weekend discussions to ask questions. For example, the two leaders wanted to know how people felt about living in big and small cities and whether their opinion of apartments would change if they could spend weekends and vacations in single family housing or if the apartments had private balconies large enough for some planting and outdoor relaxation.

Caruso and Grant also showed videos of new, and old, apartment houses that they thought might be acceptable, including some from outside America. One of Grant's personal favorites was a mid-twentieth-century Canadian project called Habitat. Designed by Moshe Safdie, it featured prefabricated modules of apartments with balconies that were so cantilevered that the occupants enjoyed light and openness as well as privacy from their neighbors. The original Habitat was beset by problems and may have been ahead of its time, but a redesigned and seemingly problem free version had just been built.

The O'Hara White House passed the density buck to the housing market and halted further discussions, but Gordon resumed them. She also initiated a series of modest experiments. The first experiments tested the feasibility and popularity of various suburban apartment house types, but the later ones included housing types previously associated with cities, including some from the early twentieth century such as Boston's three-deckers and even Manhattan's five-story walk-ups. Over a hundred of these were eventually built or restored in various low density locations across the country but failed to attract any enthusiasm. Only exercise buffs would choose to live on the top floor of walk-up housing.

The experimenters tested a high rise row house, twelve duplexes on top of each other around an elevator core, and a twenty-story apartment house with every fifth floor an open one with areas set aside for adults and as children's playgrounds. They also asked a sample of suburbanites to live in twenty-fifth-floor apartments in contemporary high rise buildings in New York, Chicago, and Los Angeles. Some of the suburbanites who "tested" penthouses were ready to stay, but those living temporarily in apartments liked them only as places to visit.

Actually, the most popular site was a sumptuous duplicate of Corbusier's superblock, with small tropical parks, swimming pools, and outdoor cafes between the buildings. Many people said that it felt just like a resort and they could see themselves living in it for quite awhile.

The experimenting became serious in Gordon's second term, when two large developers about to construct new light industrial facilities and offices were brought together with residential builders and persuaded with extra tax abatements to build two modest but nearly carless rental communities around their new workplaces. By now the residential developers have built a couple of apartment neighborhoods consisting mostly of six- to eight-story buildings and a few ten- to twelve-story ones located in neo-Corbusierian superblocks.

The neighborhoods are planned so as to enable workers to walk or use motorized bicycles or public jitneys to go to work. Both projects are located near shopping malls and at intersections of major highways that facilitate the in and out access needed by the firms and the residents.

The experiment will test whether or how long two sets of Americans are prepared to live in apartment houses and without their own cars. However, both projects are planned so that, if necessary, parking lots for residents' owned cars and for rented cars can be provided later at the edges of both projects.

The remaining experiments are field projects, studying how people in various kinds of low and medium density housing are coping with high energy costs and what informal solutions, if any, they have developed that could be adopted on a wider scale. The extent to which people are making personal decisions to give up their cars, depend on old or newly developed mass transit, or move to higher density housing and closer to work are also being tracked.

Even so, some planners, architects, and social scientists are already at work on paper plans for a lower energy future. One plan calls for high density at work and lower density at home. It would start from the fact that a large number of Americans outside of the biggest cities are already living, working, and shopping near expressways. If more future workplaces can be located near expressways and clustered in high rise loft and office buildings, many workers could reach them by mass transit, using jitneys, motorized bicycles, or their legs to commute between home and the nearest transit stop. Eventually, some expressways could become transitways.

In addition, so-called work malls that collect a number of workplaces might have to be located in contemporary suburban America so that a maximum number of workers will be able to reach them with a minimal expenditure of oil or other scarce energy sources. Even if residents were willing to leave their communities, the country could not afford to scrap the century-long investment in suburban low density housing.

The planners cannot yet estimate how many and what kinds of firms would be able to operate in high density workplaces. Moreover, most workers would still—and may always—be employed in low density workplaces such as small factories, offices, and stores, although in the long run those workplaces lending themselves to clustering could be brought together. The biggest challenges to density increases are the small and medium sized towns and cities in which working and living take place at low densities and that may be far from the expressway system, and the planners intend to leave them alone until energy costs or global warming reach a critical level. Meanwhile, their occupants will have to spend more of their incomes on transportation.

Unfortunately, plans can be made only by vastly oversimplifying reality and ignoring the political and economic conflicts and other obstacles to achieving them. Settling the conflicts that come with a change of the basic density and transportation structures will probably take a generation or two. Right now, the Hernandez administration has its hands full with evaluating the past experiments and conducting others, but some of the planners are already hoping for a miracle in which the increases in both energy cost and global warming will suddenly be halted.

A National Mass Transit System

Planning for a national mass transit system proceeded more quickly than planning for higher densities, because the White House decided early on to begin modestly. No one knew how many Americans would get out of their cars as gasoline prices continued to increase or whether they would do so even if presented with a state of the art system that would deposit them within eyeball distance of both job and home.

Caruso and Grant took once more to their TV program, hoping to start people thinking about the conditions under which they would use various kinds of mass transit. Soon after, the Department of Transportation began the jitney experiment. A sample of suburbs and low density cities was chosen to find out whether commuters would give up their cars if they could be picked up at the nearest street corner for a group ride, either to work or to a nearby express bus or commuter train.

The experiment killed several birds with one stone, for Detroit's big cars would serve nicely as jitneys. Until the system paid for itself, the global warming jobs program could hire both the part-timers who would drive jitneys at rush hours and the full-timers who would provide more restricted service during the rest of the day.

The jitney experiment was successful when fully used so that it could be cheap enough for riders to leave cars at home. Where it was made permanent, it often turned into a car pool service, the same five or six commuters using it daily. Vans and even small buses replace the jitneys when the number of riders to be picked up is large enough. Whether such a system is economically feasible and reduces energy use sufficiently remains to be seen and probably depends on how many people can be persuaded to give up their private cars.

Meanwhile, mass transit systems are being built or rebuilt all over the country, the pace depending not only on the availability of public funds but also on indications that the systems will be used. The old chicken-egg debates continue, but the mass transit fans who argue that riders will come when the systems are built have to provide better evidence before scarce resources can be allocated. Moreover, if the nonpolluting automobile engine can be built, the riders will stop coming.

Most of the existing and new bus and train systems are or will eventually be electric. In some places, people still remembered the electric trolleys and trolley busses that had provided public or tourist transportation in the twentieth century. Since the mass transit system has to be as user friendly as possible, trolleys are supplied even when they are not economic or increase congestion. Gordon was a particularly energetic trolley booster, and she even pressed for monorails, which she thought of as high speed trolleys.

Gordon's Secretaries of Energy and of Transportation encouraged the expansion of ferries to transport commuters and others in communities located on or near lakes, rivers, and other waterways, including some bays and oceans. Today, the ferries are being replaced by high speed electrified boats and hydrofoils with batteries that can be recharged during off-hours.

The local ground systems are or will be connected to a parallel national railroad system that might someday span the country again. Dreamers in the Department of Transportation are even talking about lobbying for an intercontinental TGV ([*train à grande vitesse*] high speed train) and trying to design a TGV freight system that could replace some of the giant trucks used for very long distance transportation of goods. Barges are another possible replacement for some of the huge trucks. Currently, there is talk about TGVs and other fast trains replacing some airline routes. Airplanes consume a great deal of fossil fuel, although national and international tourism are economically too essential to do away with the huge planes that make it possible.

Mass transit can be put into service on expressways that originally had been built with or had retained median easements usable for rails. Now that cars are small enough that expressway lanes can be narrowed, one or two lanes can even be diverted to high speed rail or monorail service. Some ferry enthusiasts even propose turning highway easements into narrow waterways that can accommodate small ferries.

Superfluous Places

During Gordon's second term, the Secretary of Energy urged her to start thinking about the future of the country's superfluous places: the nearly empty and emptying communities found all over America that are still adding to energy use and carbon dioxide emissions despite their decreased populations. Some are old cities that once were home to industries that no longer exist; others are small market and factory towns made obsolete by shopping mall cities and the departure of manufacturing. A few of these places now house old people who could not leave when the communities crashed economically, and some store economically superfluous poor people who cannot wait to get out. Other areas are unneeded farmland or literal and figurative deserts devoid of human uses or underground raw materials.

While superfluous places located near forested, mountainous, and other scenic areas should be held for future recreational use, those located in unattractive surroundings and sufficiently clustered to create sizable patches of superfluous territory might be closed down for awhile to save energy.

Washington had so long been preoccupied with economic growth that no one had thought about areas possibly being considered superfluous when energy use had to be reduced. Local opposition to being so considered also played a role. Area development grant and various earmark programs were still trying to help some of these places, but resuscitating a dying community is a thankless if not impossible task—and all the more so if the remaining residents resist change in it.

The Hernandez administration is now planning to demolish a few totally deserted small towns and neighborhoods in the emptying cities, mostly as an early way of calling attention to the problem. However, then it will have the opportunity or the burden of figuring out what to do with them.

Most of the early proposals are conventional, but the Hernandez administration is toying with a long-range scheme that is connected to energy use reduction programs. A national resettlement plan would divide the empty and near empty areas of the country into livable and unlivable ones, the latter being areas that would become too hot or too cold or both for comfortable living if and when heating and cooling costs become stratospheric.

The livable areas would be put into a federal reserve, to be held when land is needed for immediate and distant national emergencies, such as earthquakes or hurricanes that destroy entire communities. For example, should global warming actually raise ocean levels sufficiently to flood some of the country's lowest lying coastal cities, relocation communities will be needed quickly.

Given the large number of communities located on or close to the country's eastern, western, and southern coastlines, such relocation communities could require a large amount of land. Moreover, if global warming continues, the now century-long population movement to the coasts will have to end, forcing many Americans to again live inland.

The worst case analysts who believe that eventually global warming will empty some southern regions of the planet suggest that the resulting northward population movements would inevitably require access to now vacant American land and no borders could stop them. Although the global warming experts are now making short-, medium- and long-term flooding estimates for all low lying parts of the country and of the world, no one can yet make reliable predictions about the future.

So far, the Hernandez administration has not said anything about land reserve plans, but early leaks about the unlivable area designation have already evoked political protest in the many areas that have always been too hot or cold. People who have become used to living under such climatic conditions feel insulted and the livable-unlivable dichotomy will probably not survive.

Private enterprise has already been making its own land reserve plans. Rumors have circulated since the 2020s that "Wall Street," which abuts the low lying New York Bay, has bought land in the Catskills or the Adirondacks or both. Some developers who traditionally have built oceanfront mansion communities are reported to have taken some of their panicky clients to see scenic acreage in the nearest mountainous areas.

CHAPTER SIX

SCHOOLINGS

Caruso was not particularly interested in education policies, treating his Small Class Initiative primarily as a job creation scheme. He had asked the young Hernandez, who was passionately involved with education policy, to be the White House staff person on education and later appointed him Secretary of Education. Hernandez was dedicated to helping ordinary youngsters from the below median income population who would never be top students but could nevertheless benefit economically from schooling. When he was teaching school, he had met like-minded young teachers and activists working to improve schools in poor neighborhoods. As he would have readily admitted then, they gave him many of the ideas he subsequently tried out from the White House and the Department of Education.

True, Hernandez was more skeptical than the activists and his fellow teachers about what could be done. He knew that public education was often better at blocking upward mobility than aiding it.

However much it helped to push very bright and ambitious individuals from the below median income population into the middle class and beyond, public education also kept kids from that population with only ordinary talents in the parental place.

Hernandez knew too that the most effective policies to help children from low and moderate income homes to learn were not just educational. He was particularly impressed by the steady jobs hypothesis: that, all other things being equal, parents with steady jobs and economic security somehow enabled and encouraged their children to do well enough in school to also obtain steadier and better jobs—at least as long as such jobs were available. Thus, Hernandez hoped that some of Caruso's jobs and incomes programs would eventually have educational effects and that the health programs associated with the nurse-doctor project would reduce the many ailments that kept poor children out of school more often than children of better off families.

TESTING FOR TALENTS

However, Hernandez's first task as the education point man in the White House was to eliminate the last remnants of the Bush administration's No Child Left Behind program. Hernandez bitterly opposed all teaching-to-the-test programs, favored testing to the course, and urged that the department develop national courses, with accompanying tests, in several basic subjects, beginning as always with math and science. Some local school boards were pleased with the extra help, others objected, but Caruso stood solidly behind his educators.

Although the first new courses and tests focused mostly on academic skills, when Hernandez became Secretary of Education, he added others that practiced and stretched predominantly non-academic talents that students might turn into labor market skills. Among the talents he had in mind were curiosity; puzzle solving; inventing; discovering; and social talents such as inspiring, leading, and conciliating.

Other talents include verbal abilities such as articulateness and rhetorical ability, as well as political talents, including diplomacy, conflict resolution, and compromising. Subsequently a course to discourage negative talents, among them manipulation, sabotaging, double-dealing, and lying, has also been created.

Over fifteen years have passed since the start, in 2016, of what is now called Testing for Talent. Much time was spent in trial and error and dealing with spirited opposition from teachers of academic subjects. Many of the latter were won over when youngsters who excelled in the talent courses started taking a greater interest in academic courses as well.

Today, adolescents who perform at a high level in the talent courses can compete for special internships, college scholarships, and subsequent employment by private firms and public agencies. Similar talent courses are now being considered by colleges and universities.

Hernandez was especially pleased because talent testing has also achieved one of its original though less publicized purposes: to alter thinking about racial, class, and gender achievement gaps. Once achievement in nonacademic talents was measured by tests and student performance, the traditional achievement gap framework, which was excessively based on academic testing, lost some of its credibility.

As a result, a number of class, race, and gender differences thought to be due to variations in intelligence declined or disappeared. Indeed, poor youngsters often scored higher than affluent children on several talents, especially those crucial to survival in low income neighborhoods.

Moreover, once talent is defined to include more than academic talent, the notion that poor children are "culturally disadvantaged" no longer makes sense. Even though poverty continues to hold these children back, many now feel more positive about their attempts to escape it. However, the youngsters who also perform well in academic courses still walk off with the best college choices and job offers.

For a while, Hernandez had to fight strenuously to prevent his original program from being superseded by what he privately called educational gentrification, as affluent school districts demanded their share of the talent program funds. The gentrification process peaked during the O'Hara years, but after Gordon became president, citizen lobbies that represented below median income parents of high school age youngsters helped her to restore the program's original priority.

THE RELEVANCE POLICIES

Hernandez did not ignore the rest of his department's youthful constituents, including those who were not curious or motivated to learn. He believed that some students might be turned on if school were more relevant to their interests, concerns, and even anxieties. Relevance was an old but now forgotten term from the 1960s, and while he was Education Secretary, he came up with several relevance policies.

Hernandez began by arguing for courses that would add relevance to the standard offerings. Thus, he thought that history courses should be taught more to help students make sense of the present than to add to their knowledge of the past. He wanted zoology courses to help students understand the animals that they lived with, that they ate, and that sickened them.

Hernandez believed that the social sciences could be taught in part from the daily news and that some basic themes in social relations and psychology could be illustrated by the lyrics of songs currently popular with students. The classics of world literature might make more sense to students if their analysis was sometimes paired with that of currently popular fiction. Most of these course ideas were not original; in fact, many were left over from the days of progressive education.

Teaching to the Present

Hernandez tried out another relevance policy that he dreamed up when he was a young teacher. Like other teachers, he quickly realized that preteens and teens, notably poor males, often tuned out of courses that were preparing them for an adult society that appeared to have no use for them. Others seemed uninspired by the image of adulthood that their courses communicated to them.

If junior high and high school could focus less on preparing students for an uncertain adulthood and instead help them make sense of their current lives, the Hernandez thinking went, more students might trust the schools and their teachers. Then they might also be more receptive to learning some of the ideas and skills they would need in adult society.

However, what Hernandez called teaching to the present was difficult, because many teachers were unfamiliar with the preoccupations and frustrations of their young charges and relevant teaching materials were nonexistent. Then Hernandez found some teachers ready to educate themselves by asking teenagers to talk about their lives.

Eventually, the talking produced some courses. For example, social science courses used the students' experiences and problems in dealing with in and out of school student culture, including peer pressure. Economics was taught by extrapolating from the experiences of youngsters who worked as cashiers or hamburger flippers. A biology course led off by discussing teenage body image issues. An engineering course was created by and for youngsters who rebuilt junked cars or motorcycles.

One of the more successful courses taught English by building on the youngsters' need to code switch between standard English, the latest teenage expressions, and ethnic language variations like black vernacular and Spanglish. Immigrant youngsters practiced code switching with the parental language. Code switching was fun, and at least some students began to pay more serious attention to the adult mainstream language they were being taught in regular English classes.

Students as Teachers

Many former teachers in the Department of Education knew from personal experience that students learned most when they were doing the teaching themselves. As Secretary of Education, Hernandez, ready to try almost anything, asked the nation's schools to give students a chance to teach. Not all were agreeable, and teachers unions as well as staff lobbies had to agree first, but finally federal pilot programs were initiated in willing school districts.

Most of the time, brighter students tutored their weaker peers, but sometimes they led classes, for example, to help fellow students understand what they had missed when the teacher first presented the materials. Occasionally students were sent into lower grades to help teach courses they had themselves taken a few years earlier. Sometimes the more diplomatic students could even give tips to novice teachers. And a few courageous schools with too few teachers for the gifted set up courses that gave such students the needed materials and let them teach each other. However, only a handful of schools were ready to try a riskier Hernandez idea: to encourage weaker students to learn by having to teach and to try to bring dropouts back into the system the same way.

Despite its frequent pedagogical success, the student-as-teacher program often ran into political troubles. Parents were concerned that their children were being exposed to inferior instruction, and teachers resented students who made their materials clearer than they did. A scheme to treat the teaching students as interns and pay them a nominal wage raised fears that students were being used as cheap labor preliminary to cutting teacher pay. Hernandez had to do a lot of extra traveling to rescue his program from local opposition.

The Talking Program

Hernandez's best remembered innovation, which involved the Department of Education in nursery school education, may have been the talking program. Twentieth-century researchers and educators had already documented that middle class parents, particularly well educated ones, started their children's preschool education by beginning to talk *to* them not long after birth and by talking *with* them as soon as they were able to respond.

As the sociologist Annette Lareau had reported early in the twenty-first century, poorly educated parents talked to and with their children much less often and then more to maintain discipline than to stimulate their children's imaginations and satisfy their curiosity. And exhausted, troubled, or depressed parents were too preoccupied with their own problems to do more than try to control their youngsters, thereby also inhibiting the children's ability and willingness to learn.

Consequently, Hernandez proposed that day care and nursery

schools, especially in poor neighborhoods, should make time for talking sessions. He made speeches about the importance of turning on babies' talking machinery, and eventually the program became so popular that talking courses are now part of the nursery school curriculum almost everywhere.

In fact, the talking courses are such a success that some parents complain that after a long day's work, they lack the energy to meet their children's after school demands for more talking. Immigrant parents are particularly disadvantaged because they may not know the answers to their children's questions.

POLITICAL EDUCATION FOR DEMOCRACY

The night Caruso, Gordon, and Hernandez first met in 2010, they agreed that in order to flourish in an ever more complicated society, citizens would eventually have to become fully informed about the public policies and politics on which their well-being depended. In fact, they would have to know as much about them as they now know about reality television, bargain hunting, and baseball statistics. During his first campaign, a frustrated Caruso once asked why the public schools could not offer courses in these subjects.

Everyone, including Caruso, knew the answer, of course: local school boards, politicians, and some parents would be upset. Many students were not especially interested. They had learned that politics was dirty. Teachers had been taught that schools were above politics, and partisan parents would quickly object if uncomfortable facts about their party or their favorite politicians came up in class.

Nonetheless, once Hernandez became the White House staffer for education, Caruso asked him to look further into the idea and check it out with national teacher and school board organizations. Sounding out these groups and other interested parties took a long time, but when Hernandez became Secretary of Education, he suggested trying out a course on politics that would complement the conventional high school civics and social studies curricula.

Now Hernandez had to sell the idea—he called it education for democracy—to a small number of communities that would try out the new course. He especially needed to persuade the teachers in these communities, who wanted to know how they, as untrained in politics as their students, were supposed to instruct them.

Caruso stipulated that no federal funds could go into this project, but some national foundations were supportive, and they supplied funds for the pilot project. The first course was often watered down; usually the superintendent invited local elected officials and other politicians—retired ones turned out to be the best choices—to tell students about local politics. The politicians rarely spoke frankly, but sometimes inquisitive students asked such frank questions that Hernandez had to send one of his assistants to cool off local political tempers.

Ultimately, a solution was found: the self-study, in which students carried out research on the politics of their own high schools and communities. The young researchers looked not only at student politics but also at the politics of the administrations, and they investigated the hierarchies of the student social structures, how superintendents and principals led and controlled their teachers, and how the school boards related to the community power structures.

The first self-studies were primitive, but then students and their teachers dug up helpers, often from local colleges. Although Washington insisted that the purpose of the education for democracy project was to increase understanding rather than to expose politics, the studies frequently turned controversial. Here and there, teachers punished the researchers with low grades, and principals tried to suspend them. Occasionally student leaders attacked the researchers. However, the publicity generated by these reprisals and the resulting court cases evoked more interest in, and then legitimated, the self-studies. By the time Caruso left the White House self-studies were being conducted under federal auspices in high schools all across the nation.

When Gordon became president, a large number of communities reported that the self-studies were now being complemented by political education courses. Today, nearly a decade later, many schools systematically teach students about practiced politics at all levels of government. Although most students will not become politically active adults, the courses may make them sufficiently knowledgeable to realize when they need to become active.

The Schools, the News, and the Entertainment Media

The public and even the commercial news media took an early interest in the political education program. Their interest in teaching democracy was hard to gauge, but they all were eager to prepare students to become adult members of their audiences. A nationwide opportunity to do so did not often come their way.

The commercial entertainment media arrived on the scene not long after the news media. For example, game producers have come up with a series of political strategy games that allow high school students, and younger ones, to play a variety of political roles, from local district leader to U.S. president. The schools choose games that reflect the complexity involved in public decision making and stay away from those using violence to settle conflicts.

When he was Caruso's Education Secretary, Hernandez had already tried to bring the schools and the various entertainment media closer together—and with an agenda that transcended political education. Hernandez argued that many children seemed to learn more from the entertainment media than they did from media educational programming and than they did in the classroom. Consequently, the schools could only benefit from paying more attention to these media.

Hernandez's effort failed, partly because the educational establishment felt popular entertainment culture was incompatible with school culture. In addition, entertainment media firms had tried too often to invade the classroom in order to gain footholds for their advertisers.

Gordon's Department of Education, pressed both by the entertainment industry and by the citizen lobbies fighting the industry's various shortcomings, established a popular culture division. The division suggested that instead of rejecting popular culture, the schools should use it for its own purposes—and most constructively perhaps by taking it apart critically and correcting it when required.

The idea is not new, but high school humanities courses now regularly undertake literary and cultural analyses of the latest electronic and digital fare most popular among the students. Social science instructors are using the media in teaching about American society: for example, teaching about the family in part by correcting the stereo-types, simplifications, and plain inaccuracies found in the most popular family shows on television and the Internet.

While some students balked at taking apart their favorite programs, the ones who had been making fun of the shows even while watching them discovered that their irreverent reactions frequently were similar to the teachers' analyses. When student teaching became normal practice, those students volunteered most eagerly to teach the analysis courses.

UPDATING HIGHER EDUCATION

Caruso thought the colleges and universities should raise the skill levels of their students to improve the country's ability to compete for the world's best jobs. Once more he asked Hernandez to focus especially on the below median income population. Arguing that more high school graduates from that population should go to college, Hernandez came up with two programmatic ideas while he was on the White House staff.

The first was obvious to anyone living in a low or moderate income community. Even though they no longer had to pay tuition, the youngsters needed financial help for themselves or their families to be able to go to school—and to have time to study. The White House could not afford to ask Congress for further expensive programs. However, the heavily endowed private schools, which were already feeling the heat for not doing enough for the country's poor youngsters, were persuaded to provide some of the needed financial aid from their tax exempt and highly profitable endowments.

Gordon later proposed, unsuccessfully, to end the tax exemption for endowment donations to private schools, but the idea is not dead, and someday every qualified but needy high school graduate will be offered an all expenses paid public college education.

Hernandez's second idea would allow qualified youngsters to skip two years of school, either by starting college after their sophomore year in high school or by an accelerated program that combined high school and college courses. Similar programs had been established in various localities for the last century, and Hernandez viewed them as a way to rescue bright kids from poor high schools.

Not many school boards wanted to permit their young people to skip two years of high school, but Caruso liked the idea enough to put some Oval Office muscle behind it. A few communities were chosen to try out the idea. Some students went to community colleges that had room for them; others wound up at small private colleges that badly needed more students. As expected, some of the sophomores were not ready to study at college level, and others could not adjust to the college routine, but many more than expected completed the program and could enter the job market two years earlier than students with four years of high school.

Hernandez came away from the experiment wanting to invent a new community college that would be able to enroll high school sophomores, offer a year of catch-up schooling for youngsters who dropped out of high school, and even admit older dropouts who now realized they needed more education. The catch-up students, he hoped, would stay on for a second year of school or move on to a four-year college. Such a school would probably need to develop a new college culture, and students who were the first in their families to go to college might work together to create it. Perhaps some of these community colleges ought to be dormitory schools, enabling youngsters from the lower economic strata to obtain the same kind of education as their more fortunate peers.

Hernandez created a file on his computer for his ideas about these innovations, looked at them again when he was governor of New Mexico, and then examined them once more when he arrived in the White House. Perhaps he would find some young people who could try to realize them, or maybe he would do so himself once he was a former president figuring out what to do with himself for the rest of his life.

Colleges and Careers

Once he became Secretary of Education, Hernandez devoted more of his attention to the middle class students that were then, with their parents, the major constituency for higher education. Even when Hernandez himself was going to school, he had already concluded that colleges could do more to use their regular courses to help students think about careers and how to choose them. Hernandez was thinking especially of the students who could not decide what they would do after college. As a result, too many of them went off to graduate schools in which they did not belong or drifted into jobs and careers for which they were not suited.

Caruso once had made a somewhat similar point on the campaign trail and therefore gave his blessing to a presidential commission to discuss the curriculum problem. The commission's final recommendations called for the creation of a career curriculum consisting of a wide range of specially designed liberal arts courses supplemented by preprofessional ones that would together contribute to students' career quests.

Over the next decade, colleges and universities tried out many versions of the career curriculum, which soon was referred to informally as CC. The professional schools often came up with undergraduate courses promoting their professions, but the scholarly disciplines, feeling defensive, therefore had special reason to contribute relevant courses—and very few refused the invitation.

English departments taught how American literature and other literatures portrayed various careers, and the faculty at one institution was pleased to discover that a course on law and lawyers in American fiction attracted a record number of very bright, mostly pre-law students. Sociology offered new courses about the institutions, cultures, and clients that each of the major professions and other occupations served and the restraints under which these operated. Economists demonstrated the monetary and other realities behind the glossy images concocted by various professions; political scientists talked about the professions' internal and external political activities.

At the end of a decade of experimentation and trial and error innovation, President Gordon welcomed the official arrival of the career curriculum to the educational scene at a White House ceremony. She was pleased to hear that the program would blossom without significant further federal aid, and she asked whether any of its components could be adapted for high schools.

The Place of the Liberal Arts

The CCers not only helped the liberal arts faculties to raise their enrollments but also demonstrated that the career curriculum itself needed the liberal arts for intellectual depth and innovation. At the same time, the faculties were told that the liberal arts would be most useful if they could do more than advocate logical thought, critical analysis, and clear writing and instead actually train students to practice those skills. Likewise, while the liberal arts should continue to teach the best that Western and other world civilizations offer, they ought to encourage students to add to the best rather than merely understand what had already been produced.

In addition, the CC planners requested more relevance. They suggested that courses in literary analysis should regularly teach writers and thinkers whose ideas could be connected directly to current economic, social, political, and intellectual issues. Likewise, courses on political thought should teach students about current political manipulators, of power as well as of symbols, in addition to having them read Machiavelli.

If today's students could not make sense of, or fell asleep over, the ideas of ancient or medieval thinkers, required liberal arts courses might try to concentrate on modern thinkers. Interested students could learn about the important minds of the past in elective courses.

Selling Collegiate Sports

In one of their reports to the White House, the national CC planners observed that too few collegiate athletes were being prepared for meaningful future careers. Their matter of fact observation gave Hernandez, as Caruso's Education Secretary, an excuse to propose for perhaps the thousandth time that something be done about the structural shortcomings of college athletics that the many reform attempts had not eliminated.

Despite Hernandez's cabinet position, the athletic powers that be put him off with new commissions and further studies. However, after Gordon became president, she put pressure on the major national organizations of higher education. Then she called the presidents and coaches of the schools with the most extensive and profitable athletic programs to a meeting in the White House. Soon thereafter, and following some prompting from politically influential alumni, the presidents and coaches were persuaded to agree, in writing, that colleges and universities should not be in the business of entertaining the world outside the campus and that their sports facilities ought henceforth to be used for physical education, student exercise, and intramural athletics.

Noting that in many sports, collegiate teams were de facto training camps and minor leagues for the professional major leagues, the school presidents and coaches agreed further that such teams be sold to their local communities or to the alumni that were already supporting them. The current leagues and divisions could be transformed into professional minor leagues or franchised to national and international sports conglomerates.

The schools had much to sell or rent: their names, their stadia, and their gyms, as well as the virtually captive audiences that many attracted for major sports. Consequently they could demand a healthy percentage of the ticket, television, and Internet sales for major sporting events and for games in some of the minor sports. Women's tennis appeared to be a particularly attractive crowd pleaser at the moment. Although many alumni grumbled about losing "their teams," and some local and state politicians threatened legislation to block any such scheme, college administrations, coaches, faculty, and students generally were pleased by the recommendations.

The coaches expected increased salaries, and the top players looked forward to earning more than their coaches. Freed from participating in schoolwork for which they never had sufficient time, they could devote themselves to additional training, and more of them might eventually move up to the professional major leagues. A much larger number could expect a minor league career that lasted more than the three or four years they would have played on college teams. They could even study part-time while they were players and become full-time students after their playing days ended.

Despite Gordon's enthusiastic support for the professionalization of college sports, the process spread slowly across the country and the various sports during the rest of the 2020s. Ironically enough, President Hernandez was said to be miffed because public attention to his inauguration was diverted by rumors that several Big Ten football teams were about to be sold as franchises of a multinational sports corporation.

Coping with New Educational Technologies

Besides overcoming various financial crunches, higher education has also had to adapt to new technologies. Of course, so have all other large organizations, but the college campus has had a distinctive duo of constituencies: a young one, most of them ready to embrace the latest technologies; and an older one, many of them still accustomed to early-twenty-first-century technologies and unwilling to update their technical training every few months.

Reading remains the fundamental learning method, but most students read only texts that appear on their All Purpose Personal Communicators (APPCs). Although the undergraduates still often study in library reading rooms, most of the books that are still issued on paper are taken out by the faculty and some graduate students.

Partly as a result, universities have long been trying to figure out what to do about their libraries and their books. Many have already joined one of the large regional libraries that deliver books over a wide area. Then they downsize their own library and use the savings to hire more reference librarians and information specialists. Many of the downsized libraries retain only their reading rooms and a book and journal display area, the rest of their building being converted into offices, housing, and student study-and-coffee lounges. Students and teachers who prefer to browse in the library stacks instead of the Internet's virtual ones can obtain free transportation to the nearest regional library.

The future of the campus classroom is also under discussion. Most of the bigger schools still try to maximize large enrollment courses, with a single professor addressing 250 or more students and a host of young instructors and graduate students leading small discussion sections. But today the lecturer can also be heard and seen on the APPCs, and only extraordinary performers attract a physically present student audience of respectable size.

As a result, schools increasingly are replacing their large lecture courses with video presentations delivered by nationally known professors, most of them at the country's premier research universities or selective colleges. Some are even freelancing celebrities. Many of the professors that once lectured to large classes prefer to teach smaller ones anyway.

Faculty Changes

By 2020, Caruso's small classes program had made an impression on the thinking in higher education circles, and by the end of the decade, small classes, many of them discussion sessions, outnumbered the larger lecture courses nearly everywhere, except at public colleges in financial difficulties.

Much of the increase in costs was borne by the faculty. Adjuncts now teach a higher proportion of the regular courses, especially in the classes devoted to transmitting information that needs little discussion. Although adjuncts are not expected to publish, they are often better teachers than the regular faculty. Since the proportion of courses taught by adjuncts counts heavily in professional evaluations of school quality and reputation, however, the most selective and most expensive schools restrict the number of adjuncts.

Despite endless attacks on tenure, it has survived. However it is now often awarded only to the best known, most important, and most prolific faculty members. Everyone else is on contracts, eight years still for assistant professors but ten years and longer for the higher ranks. Adjuncts usually receive five-year contracts. Although few professors are ever fired, deadwood faculty usually find themselves with five-year contracts, and if they do not work harder subsequently, they are offered only adjunct contracts. In many schools, performance requirements have been tightened and raised over the last quarter century, although after professors reach age fifty-five, they are relaxed again until people retire.

Except at unionized schools, salary increases have become more modest, in part because smaller classes officially are deemed to require less work. Conversely, adjuncts are now paid more than the day labor wages of the past.

Thanks to the twentieth-century struggles in behalf of academic freedom and in exchange for the reduction in tenured positions, all teaching contracts, including those of adjuncts, carry a guarantee of academic freedom. Thus, even the most insistent state legislators or political lobbies cannot bring about the termination of faculty intellectual or political dissidents. To be sure, they remain vulnerable to being let go for alleged or real violations of campus regulations, including those never before enforced.

The Two Track Faculty

Several universities that are or aspire to become research universities currently are carrying out a long talked about faculty division of labor between teaching and research professors. Researchers will no longer have to earn their livings by spending most of their time teaching, and teachers who want to be in the classroom will not have to publish only to prevent perishing. The so-called two track system is flexible, however, for when slots are available, faculty members can move from one to the other and back again.

Faculty can also remain in the traditional system, combining teaching and research. The old system works best in fields that rarely receive outside research funding and in those in which researchers make their contributions early in their careers and then turn to teaching. In addition, all faculty members are free to do what they want during the time when they are not actually teaching or researching.

To enhance flexibility and advance equality, the two tracks are similar in many respects, with the same ranks, pay scales, and promotion standards. Graduate students all take the same substantive courses in their fields, but those who already know they want to teach become discussion leaders or substitute teachers rather than research assistants. Instead of writing dissertations, they develop two or three new courses, teach them once, and revise them following evaluations from mentors and students. Students preparing to spend their lives mainly as researchers continue to be trained in the traditional pattern, writing publishable research papers and dissertations for their doctoral degrees.

Career researchers are hired with the same contracts as teaching professors, and universities must guarantee their salaries even if the funding comes from "soft" or temporary grant monies. In the long run, such parity is too expensive; as a result, research funding agencies are now being asked to pay for the tenure or long-term contracts of the research professors who guide much of their research. One salutary result: professors with job security are less likely to work concurrently for commercial firms that can generate conflicts of interest. Conversely, faculty not assured of job security are more likely to work for the firms than in the past.

Interdisciplinary Scholarship

The gradual formation of a research professoriat has had at least one surprising effect: the emergence of actually existing rather than imagined interdisciplinary research. Most of the natural sciences were already removing arbitrary historic boundaries before the end of the last century, but in the humanities and social sciences, the individual disciplines had long ago marked their territories and fortified their borders against outsiders. For example, they typically used different frameworks, concepts, and reading lists even when they were asking the same research questions or teaching the same subjects.

The public and commercial funders of research have little patience with disciplinary borders; they want problems solved and questions answered. University administrations see interdisciplinary departments as a way to reduce overhead costs. As a result, an increasing number of research universities have been combining departments. Some Economics and Political Science departments have been united as departments of Political Economy; Sociology, Anthropology, and Social Psychology have come together as Social Relations, or, if they also merge with one or more life sciences, they call themselves departments of Biosocial Relations. Sometimes departments that combine disciplines adopt novel names that can be trademarked and displayed in university advertising.

A few pioneering schools even have added history to the combine. Hopeful administrators believe this union will revive historical interest in theory and method and encourage the social relations faculty to imitate the historians' ability to write clear English. After some years of intellectual and other power struggles, the frequently forced marriages have begun to pay off with new ideas, concepts, research projects, and courses. The willingness of governmental and private research funders to give priority to proposals from interdisciplinary departments has helped as well.

During their rocky phases, the disciplinary partnerships received further help from a foundation funded effort to create a technical language dictionary that will define the major terms used by every scholarly discipline and will also keep track of interdisciplinary concepts. Since the editors will identify the duplication of terms for the same concepts within and across disciplines, the dictionary may encourage its users to standardize their language when they are talking about the same thing. However, first the disciplines and faculty promotion committees must cease rewarding the creation of additional neologisms, and publishers must refuse to publish articles and books with unnecessarily technical language.

SPREADING PUBLIC INTELLECTUALS

The changes in higher education have not been limited to the campus but have spilled out over its borders. Perhaps as a result of the ever rising number of young Americans who have ventured inside those borders and graduated from college, selected members of its faculty increasingly have ventured out beyond the campus. Although they should probably be called public professors, they are known, rightly or wrongly, as public intellectuals.

To be sure, professors able and willing to offer analytic and critical commentary on the country's cultural, political, and other issues for the better educated general public have been around for many years. Until the middle of the last century, they were mostly essayists trained in literature, history, and philosophy and generally made their living outside the academy, but since then they have been joined by natural and social scientists of all kinds.

The number of public intellectuals began to increase around the start of this century, and by now professors who can communicate with the better educated general public are more visible outside the campus than in the past. Part of that influence comes from sheer mass: there are more of them in the universities; they appear more often on the op-ed pages and in general magazines as well as on television and the Internet. They are more frequently quoted by journalists, politicians, and bloggers, and many do their own blogging. The most widely seen are called celebrity profs and are photographed with entertainers who pursue intellectual interests.

Only a few people can make a living as public intellectuals, and most remain academics, but the greater presence of public intellectuals has also been transforming higher education. University administrators like public intellectuals on their faculty: they bring publicity; attract better students and faculty; and demonstrate to alumni, legislators, and trustees that professors are making public contributions that they can understand. Thus, they are often trotted out during fund-raising campaigns.

However, these intellectuals initially were less welcome inside the academic departments and professional schools. Researchers who are trained to communicate to an audience of peers and teachers who come to life in the classroom do not appreciate colleagues who spend many of their working hours with nonacademics.

Over time, however, the departments realized that PIs, as they are now often called, could increase their budgets, and faculty members became aware of their higher salaries and outside income. Partly as a result, faculty hiring rules no longer require, for example, candidates to have published only peer reviewed papers in academic journals. A prospective faculty member's number of Web site hits is sometimes more important than his or her number of publications.

The White House has watched the flowering of the PIs with nervous interest. Caruso kept his distance from them, fearing that he would be hurt politically by being too friendly to them, but Hernandez was already eager to pick their brains when he was Secretary of Education. O'Hara and Gordon regularly invited them to private White House and Camp David discussions that sometimes turned exceedingly heated. Overly critical PIs were practically assured of being invited back—to provide them with an incentive not to air their critical thoughts in the media.

In addition, PIs are often consulted by high level cabinet officials, some of whom become PIs themselves once they leave public life. Still, how much the cabinet officials—and, for that matter, presidents—listen to the PIs remains to be seen, although so far PIs have nowhere near the influence on America's public life that they have exerted in other parts of the world.

Indeed, despite the PIs' apparent glamour, most of them occupy insecure thrones, for ultimately the public decides whether it is willing to be their audience, and audiences are fickle. So are the journalists who are the major gatekeepers, and as a result PIs and especially the departments in which they teach are creating bridges with their journalism or communication schools. The bridges promise mutual benefits: the PIs can teach journalists to become better analysts while the journalists can help the PIs learn to be more topical and thus more relevant to their public audiences.

Needless to say, the public intellectuals are already far more topical than their faculty colleagues. However, as they cut a wider swath in the larger society, they are becoming popular role models for these colleagues. In the long run, it is possible that the public intellectuals' major contribution will be to the university itself, by making higher education more relevant to the country.

Some PIs are now trying to expand their audience beyond the well educated public, moving down the cultural pecking order into the mass media and onto the more popular Internet sites. These audiences require very different intellectuals: people who can translate their knowledge and insights into the formats, languages, and brevity of popular culture. Some PIs hope that, if they can accomplish these translations but still apply their analytic skills, the country someday may think a little differently about itself and the world.

Indeed, many PIs see their purpose as enhancing popular cosmopolitanism. They would like to reinforce Enlightenment values in the larger culture and encourage more cultural and political reflexivity in the general population. However, so far the PIs have not made significant inroads on the unreflexive mind-set that typifies many Americans, even those who have spent four years in college.

CHAPTER SEVEN

DEMOCRATIZING THE POLITY

I have left to the end of this history what may be in the longer historical perspective the most significant innovation of the first third of the century: the Democracy Project (DP) and its continuing activities in democratizing the country.

When the DP was established in 2012, it described itself as a floating crap game of a think tank, but today it is less irreverent. It still consists of a small staff and a larger number of volunteer researchers, brainstormers, and activists. Many are the usual assortment of bright young people ranging from dreamers to ambitious careerists that have always come to Washington. Also, the DP sometimes hires additional people for individual projects that are later spun off if they are successful. Some of the subsidiary staffs have been sizable, for example, those carrying out the DP's media activities.

However, some of the DP's most significant ideas and proposals have originated with its citizen branch, which consists of a changing and numerically never static array of people of all ages, not all of them even citizens or green card holders. They are connected to the DP by all forms of communication known to humans, and they send in ideas and comments all the time.

Formally, the DP is ideologically neutral, but its concern with democracy attracts mostly liberals. However, it seeks out others from all over the political spectrum. It also receives regular input from politicians, most of them Democratic but some Republicans and even a few libertarians.

The DP's seeds were planted early in George W. Bush's first term, when many people began to worry seriously about the future of American democracy. Once one wing of one party controlled both houses of Congress and was moving toward control of the federal courts, the vaunted American system of checks and balances showed its Achilles heel: the government could easily be turned into a one party state. The Rove strategy of a permanent Republican majority, the Cheney theory of the unitary executive, Bush's use of signing statements to veto congressional decisions, and a gerrymandered Congress in which most incumbent representatives were guaranteed regular reelection created fears that a one party state could even become a dictatorship. Some old people even remembered a 1980 book by the economist Bertram Gross entitled *Friendly Fascism*.

These and other fears led to an array of concerned foundations and think tanks, one of which hosted the conference at which Caruso, Hernandez, and Gordon first met. As noted earlier (in chap. 1, "2033 and Before"), that array then became the Tiny Liberal Conspiracy (TLC). Its participants called for the redemocratization of the country, and they set up the DP to assist in the task. Over time, however, DPers who argued that representative democracy had never been fully achieved in the United States took over the organization and broadened its mandate to furthering the country's democratization.

Officially, the DP is classified as an NGO, but unofficially, it relates to government in two ways. Typically, the DP produces policy proposals and other ideas that government may take up, sometimes only in trial balloon form. However, sometimes elected and appointed officials send ideas to the DP either for further study or testing or sometimes only to have them released as DP ideas. The losing side in a policy argument inside the government may leak its ideas to the DP, hoping that these ideas will then see the light of day with the DP's imprimatur.

In the last two decades, each branch of government has also called for the DP's abolition, especially when the organization stepped on their toes or earned the hostility of influential interests, from multicontinental corporations to the big citizen lobbies. Still, even the DP's opponents know that if it had to close shop, it would soon reappear under another name. Democracy needs a permanent nudge to keep it on its toes.

The DP has worked mainly in three areas: (1) electoral reform, to make voting easier, more attractive to citizens, and more democratic; (2) governmental structure changes, to reform undemocratic structures and remove inequalities in representation, and (3) citizen empowerment, to strengthen citizen representation beyond voting. These activities have now climaxed in an attempt to amend the Constitution to fit the country's needs in the twenty-first century.

A THEORY OF DEMOCRACY

Not long after the DP's formation, one of its academics began to work on a theory of democracy that would provide a base for the DP's three activity areas. The DP publicists simplified her paper into what they call a private-public, double world theory of democracy, and although this theory has been updated over the years, it is still used when the DP presents itself at schools, at political seminars, and to the organizations that constitute civil society.

The theory rests on the distinction between private and public worlds. It argues that most Americans live in a private world dominated by intimate and informal relations, an everyday world of families; friends; and other strong relations, such as neighbors and work colleagues.

The public world is composed of formal and bureaucratized organizations, economic, social, religious, cultural—and of course political. People who are comfortable in the private world are often uncomfortable in the public world and enter it mainly out of necessity.

It provides the jobs and services that support their private world but is otherwise shunned as a hostile culture.

Citizens are supposed to participate in the political organizations of the public world, but even many of those who vote only pay intermittent attention to politics. Although their political behavior is called political apathy, which is treated as a disease or moral failing, it is really the same avoidance behavior that is applied to the rest of the public world.

People ride bicycles and drive cars, but they do not participate in governing the companies that make them. Admittedly, they are not expected or urged to do so. Also, democratic government is not an automobile factory, but citizens may have fewer positive feelings for government than for the factory that builds their favorite cars. Besides, the political world has little more use for citizen input on governance—other than during election campaigns and those few minutes at election time—than the typical automaker has for its buyers.

Consequently, anyone seeking to further democratize the country must assume that any participation other than voting should not be expected from most people. Citizens will involve themselves actively only when they are in dire need of government services or intensely angry at politicians. Thus, further democratization must depend largely on elected officials.

For one thing, elected representatives have to be more effective representatives of their constituents, even those constituents who do not vote. Therefore, mechanisms need to be put into place to protect elected representatives from undue pressure from the "special" interests of the public world. These special interests may also be constituents, but they should not receive unfair attention or resources. Sometimes, too, elected representatives need to take the initiative and act unilaterally in behalf of democratization, but they must give the citizenry a chance to veto their actions. The second Bush often acted unilaterally but for undemocratic ends and without letting anyone veto him. No one wants to see that happen again.

The theory ends with three conclusions that justify the DP's main activities. One is the need for electoral reform, including campaign finance reform. A second is democratizing government structures through legislation; court decisions; and, if necessary, constitutional change. The third is for citizens to empower themselves by recruiting as much support as they can get, notably from social movements and citizen lobbies and even from the feedback supplied by pollsters.

Academic political theorists were not impressed with the DP's theorizing, but it served the organization's aims. The theory was most effective when politicians borrowed from it and ran with the policies and programs the DP attached to it.

ELECTORAL REFORMS

Just before Caruso's first midterm election, he initiated some citizen friendly voting experiments suggested by the DP. For example, a sample of communities turned the weekend before the election into a holiday of musical, theatrical, and other performances as well as parties.

In some places, these special events were open only to people who could provide evidence that they had already cast their ballots at nearby voting booths. In other communities, shopping malls offered prizes and discounts to voters, and tourist agencies reduced prices on postelection holidays in the sun or the snow. Some states that permitted gambling even provided voting booths in their casinos.

Also, voting booths are scattered around in groceries, drugstores, and coffee shops during election week. Election time parties are still being held, although they do not seem to raise voter participation. In a country with a fragile economy and in a fragile world, many people know they have a direct interest in and may have to depend on a competent government. Today, that is a potent incentive to vote.

The DP talked the Caruso administration into experimenting with protest ballots that enabled voters to indicate when they found all candidates wanting and with other ballots that allowed voters to indicate the reasons for their discontent. Later, O'Hara gave his support to a contentment ballot in which people could express their support of the status quo. Although polls are a better measure of voter discontent or contentment, enough people like the idea of letting off steam on the ballot to continue the experiments.

Today, efforts to get people to the ballot box are becoming quaint, for with every election, more vote by mail. Experiments with Internet voting are proceeding, and once all the digital bugs are fully removed, and protections against vote stealing and tampering can be fully guaranteed, nearly everyone may vote on the Internet.

Open Elections

In the era before voting by mail became commonplace, all three administrations tried various ways to assure open, obstacle-free elections and supervised counting of all ballots. Since many of the violations of open elections took place in poor neighborhoods, however, the Republicans were sometimes less eager to end them than the Democrats. In fact, many political historians believe that if past elections had been totally open, the Democrats might never have lost control of the Congress in the mid-1990s and its liberal wing might have been stronger as well over the last quarter century or more.

With help from the State Department, Gordon asked the United Nations to send observers to election districts with the worst voting and ballot counting records. The move created a major political explosion, Republicans accusing Democrats of putting more trust in foreigners than in Americans. However, having the United Nations look into American shortcomings for a change created some goodwill for both the United Nations and the United States.

The DP asked Congress to establish the rest of the week after election Tuesday for checking out Election Day incidents as well as mail ballots and voting machine paper trails before final votes could be officially reported. Federal election officials conducted simulated follow-up elections and then a handful of real ones in districts in which proof of sufficient election violations could be supplied.

The DP's conception of open elections included opening them up to as many people as possible. Consequently, they pressed the Supreme Court to nationalize the voting rights of ex-felons. The Court did so shortly after Gordon's first term, and since then the Democrats have worked diligently, especially in the states that contributed the largest number of people to the prison population, to make sure that they would be able to vote. Hernandez has already asked Congress to extend voting privileges to incarcerated prisoners with good behavior records.

Knowing that most prisoners will vote Democratic, the Republicans are intensely opposed. So are the small towns in which prisons are often located, for the residents do not want prisoners voting in their communities. Many prisoners feel the same way, and the eventual compromise will likely require that they vote in their home communities.

The DP is currently reintroducing a proposal it has made several times before: to let all immigrants who are not or not yet citizens vote with a special ballot. The results would not be included in the official vote, but the DP has always felt that being able to vote would encourage more immigrants to become citizens.

Campaign Finance Reform

The Bush administration's attacks on democracy as well as the still constantly rising campaign expenditures finally gave a new shot in the arm to campaign finance and related reforms. The DP persuaded Caruso to use public sentiment in favor of these reforms to argue that eventually all elections should be publicly financed. The general public might be willing to put up public funds when it was more favorably inclined toward politicians.

Still, until the courts reversed *Buckley v. Valeo* and ruled that freely spent campaign money was not free speech, Caruso and his successors had to be realistic. Consequently, Caruso proposed only that the proportion of public financing of campaigns rise 10 percent every two years and that private spending decline by an equivalent proportion, hoping thereby also to cap total spending. Congress cut the proportion to 5 percent, shot the capping idea full of loopholes, and then supported the proposal but only for presidential campaigns. Hernandez has vowed to go one step further, levying a modest but involuntary election tax on all tax payers so that they pay for a share of the campaigns. Some nonvoting taxpayers might then even decide to vote.

None of the changes totally exclude "special" interests, including the economically powerful. These organizations and persons can still spend their monies on indirect advertising and other forms of de facto campaigning, and few elected officials are yet prepared to make them stop.

Although many DPers were unhappy with this outcome, both Caruso and Gordon were satisfied. They thought that campaign advertising was becoming less effective with every election, for the political Web sites, the citizen videos, and the other "homemade" political advertising were offsetting the work of the professionals. By 2016, the amateurs'—and comedians'—satires of the professional ads were so damning that both parties and their candidates cut back advertising budgets and spent most of their money getting out the vote.

The DP also believed that the mass media that received federal support, whether through the use of public airwaves and cyberspace or subsidized postage rates, should supply a to-be-negotiated amount of free campaign advertising between Labor Day and Election Day. When the media balked, the DP sued, using eminent domain law to require the mass media to comply. The suit asked only for a limited period of free advertising during the primary season and after the World Series, but both parties loved the idea.

Lawyers doubted that land development law could be applied to communications, but the media and Web site owners blinked first. They agreed to supply the time and space the DP suit called for if they could charge off the normal price of their ads as a tax deductible cost of doing business. After the 2016 election, Congress went along with their request.

Actually, harsh realism undergirded the media's apparent cave-in, for homemade political advertising was already depressing their receipts from the political campaigns. For the media, the tax relief they received was a net profit.

The candidates were pleased, for most disliked the fund-raising needed to pay for political advertising. The journalists were pleased because they were able to take over some of the informational functions that political ads had served. The general public was particularly pleased, because the availability of free advertising and the gradual availability of public financing discouraged the parties and the candidates from buying television and Web ads. As a result, the long election campaigns became less intensive and thus easier to follow—or ignore.

During the 2032 campaign, several candidates, Hernandez included, even suggested that henceforth election campaigning should be limited to the election year and campaigning for the presidential and congressional elections should begin on Labor Day. If their suggestion is adopted, "testing the waters" and other kinds of informal campaigning will undoubtedly continue, but the daily print, electronic, and digital headlines, as well as the TV and Web site ads, will disappear, and they will not be missed.

Only the corporations, lobbies, fat cats, and others who paid for the political advertising were displeased with the availability of free campaign advertising, because the candidates were now less dependent on their funds. As a result, the funders lost some of their influence with the candidates. However, they then put more pressure on their lobbyists to deliver for them once elections were over, which not only increased the number of lobbying jobs but also helped to give rise to new citizen lobbies.

Elected officials, political observers, and even large parts of the public know that the decline of paid political advertising, the gradual increase of public financing, and the shortening of elections alone will not bring about a significant rearrangement of power in America. Businesses big and small and all other formal organizations need government more directly and immediately than most citizens. Even the now less needed campaign funders still have sufficient economic and political clout to obtain attention in Washington, but they can no longer exert quite the same amount of influence on elected officials.

In addition, the business community and others retain the built-in power that comes with providing jobs, contributing to the gross national product, and making the economy function. Big firms and even small ones can threaten to move their operations to other states, and footloose employers can threaten to leave the country or can play off communities and countries against one another.

Firms tied to their location can find executives friendly with federal and local officials, and organizations that want something from government can usually buy better information and more argumentation to support their demands than the citizenry. Nonetheless, citizen lobbies and other representatives of the citizenry can make inroads on the power of money and force elected representatives to listen to their constituencies.

Campaign Rhetoric Cleanup

Even before the DP had been organized, the Tiny Liberal Conspiracy was trying to curb the deceptive and dishonest rhetoric as well as the outright lying associated with campaigning and other political speechmaking. The TLC argued that a variety of governmental and other watchdogs was making progress in cleaning up ads that sold products and services; consequently, politics should be required to head in the same direction.

The politicians were not enthralled; they knew that political ideas and policies were harder to sell than soap. More important, diverse as well as conflict-ridden constituencies required vague rhetoric and occasional shadings of the literal truth, when one truth could be agreed on, but no one running for office could afford to oppose honesty in advertising.

In 2014, the DP set to work on an honesty drive and then spent two excruciatingly difficult years discussing the nature of truth and formulating realistic standards of accuracy and honesty for political ads and speeches with philosophers, ethicists, politicians, and campaign strategists. Having developed a grading system, the DP tested it out in the 2016 election and in 2018 developed a Web site and weekly television program that graded the campaign ads then being shown.

An audience of respectable size watched a set of masked graders, most of them editorial writers and political analysts, affix grades to the most widely shown ads, followed by often lively discussions to explain the grades. By the 2020s, the grading system was applied to regular political speeches, responses at press conferences, and even the daily pronouncements of presidential press secretaries.

The programs and Web sites that report the grading attract only small audiences, but they have stimulated many discussions and even some lawsuits over the years and in the process have also created public support for improving the level of political honesty. In addition, politicians now feel freer to admit that they do not have answers to all questions and solutions for all problems, and they explain when they have to talk in vague generalities.

Concurrently, political analysts and journalists feel free to accuse the politicians of lying, and even the president is not exempt from such accusations. In the process, the quasi monarchical deference with which the occupant of the Oval Office traditionally has been treated is eroding. At the same time and perhaps as a result, voter trust in the president and in politicians generally is now on the rise.

Admittedly, desperate and risk taking candidates occasionally try to revive the use of negative ads. Other forms of "dirty" politics have survived as well, and some observers think these have increased as political advertising was cleaned up. The next challenge, and perhaps the hardest, is to persuade voters to reject inaccurate facts when agreement on accurate ones is available and to give up unsupported beliefs they would like to hold on to.

GOVERNMENT STRUCTURAL CHANGE

The DP's second area of activity is an effort to change government structures in order to strengthen some aspects of representative democracy. The Caruso and Gordon administrations kept their distance from the DP when it was working on government change. They and, to a much lesser extent, the O'Hara administration only stepped in when legislation had to be proposed and passed and when its sponsors could receive some political credit from the DP's work.

The Small States Problem

Since the DP was first organized, it has sought to eradicate constitutional obstacles to representative democracy. Of these, the most prominent is the ability of the Electoral College to overturn the popular vote for the presidency; the other and more critical one is the undue power of the small states in the Senate.

When the DP first tackled constitutional obstacles to democracy, eliminating the Electoral College was high on the priority list. Because so few candidates have moved into the White House with a lower popular vote than the losers, the issue has slowly declined in urgency. Moreover, by now, the proposal that state legislatures require their electors to vote for the candidate winning the national popular vote has been approved by enough states to guarantee that the winner of the nation's popular vote will move into the Oval office. Obtaining that approval took much time and political energy, many Republican states refusing even to think about giving their electoral votes to the Democrats—and vice versa.

Even while the DP was trying to put the Electoral College out of business, it also got behind a long-standing effort to democratize the Senate. That effort has sought to reduce the ability of a handful of sparsely populated small states to vote against the wishes of a much larger number of people in the big states. Thanks to some long ago compromises by the nation's founders, a dozen or so small states sometimes cast the same number of votes in the Senate as the handful of large states in which most Americans live.

Some strategists believe that the small states frustrate the will of the large ones infrequently enough that permanent change is unnecessary. Instead, they suggest that when a coalition of small state senators can defeat legislation sought by the larger states, an automatic filibuster should be called. Presumably both small and large states would sit down together and use logrolling and other compromise mechanisms to induce some senators to switch their votes.

The DP has also discussed five other solutions to the small state/large state problem. In years when the biggest states have large majorities in both houses of Congress, they might be able to write legislative and appropriations bills that apply only to states of a specified minimum size, thus excluding the smaller states. Even the threat of such a maneuver might persuade some small state senators to support their big state colleagues.

Another suggestion has big state senators keeping small state colleagues out of decision-making positions on major committees and subcommittees. This idea is not taken seriously, because the Senate decision-making process is built on collegial relations and reciprocity agreements that sometimes cross party lines.

The third idea is to encourage the federal government to enable some of the smaller states to grow, for example, by supplying them with economic development and moving allowance funds to invite additional residents. Another thought is to convince some small states to merge or to share senators, but under what conditions any of the small states would consent is hard to predict. A further idea, to change the boundaries of all states so that they are reasonably equal in population, would not violate Article V of the Constitution but surely would generate unsurmountable opposition from the states that would have to be shrunk.

A fourth possibility is based on the periodically expressed desire of some larger cities to secede from their states. If New York, Chicago, Los Angeles, Philadelphia, and a handful of other cities or metropolitan areas could become separate states, the Senate would suddenly look different and therefore vote differently. Democrats might welcome such states and their normally large Democratic majorities, but few people believe secession is politically realistic or economically viable in a foreseeable future.

The DP's fifth scheme would reorganize the Senate by population size. Each state would begin with one senatorial seat and would receive additional seats equivalent to its proportion of the country's total population. A simpler version of the fifth idea would introduce fractional voting into the Senate. Then the two senators from each state would share a vote equal to their state's proportion of the total population.

All of these proposals are currently fanciful. However, if an amended Constitution argues that the one person one vote principle justifies introducing fractional voting in the Senate, the courts would have to decide whether the Founders really intended to favor the small states permanently. If not, the Senate could be reorganized to make representative democracy more egalitarian.

The Safe Seats Problem

Representative democracy has been distorted in another way by the systematic gerrymandering of election districts. Safe seats assure the availability of experienced representatives in every new Congress, but voters opposing nearly permanent incumbents claim they are being disenfranchised. Some want independent bodies to redraw district boundaries after every Census; others argue for computer drawn square or rectangular boundaries.

The political parties like safe seats since they do not have to be contested, making an otherwise unpredictable political process more predictable and allowing the parties to distribute their campaign funds where they are most needed. Although representatives in safe seats are freer to do what they think is best for the country, they are also freer to do what they want, including selling or renting themselves to the economically powerful.

Judging by the large number of people who say they like their own representative even when they mistrust the Congress as a whole, some voters may favor the familiar faces that come with safe seats. Independents argue that such seats marginalize them more than anyone else, and as their proportion of the total vote continues to grow, their complaints may be heard. But racial minorities might be unhappy if their own safe seats are eliminated. Consequently, constitutional lawyers are now discussing how to limit the parameters of permissible gerrymandering, hoping thereby to minimize the number of long-term safe seats. A one person one vote amendment to the Constitution could force the Supreme Court to decide that many gerrymanders are unconstitutional.

Limiting Executive Power

From the beginning, the DP was determined to figure out how to limit the unilateral power of presidents to hurt large numbers of people, through war making, through destructive economic policies, and in other ways. At the same time, however, no one wanted to inhibit the president's ability to act quickly and decisively for security or other reasons when necessary.

Caruso and Gordon agreed in principle with the DP, and Gordon's attorney general tried to convince the federal courts to consider declaring the Bushist theory of the "unitary executive" unconstitutional. Still, everyone sitting in the Oval Office opposed limiting the president's power in practice. For a while, Gordon was so upset with the DP that she barred its staffers from the White House.

The first implementation of the DP's two stage proposal for initiating wars occurred in the first Gordon administration. As I reported in chapter 3, "Moving toward World Peace and Planetary Survival," Congress voted that legislation to make war would have to be approved twice by both houses of Congress (and, at the second vote, by the Supreme Court) before the White House could order the Pentagon to act. The president retained the right to set aside the second stage of voting (and, with the Supreme Court's approval, even the first stage) if the country was under attack or to deal with other specified emergencies.

The DP believes that the two stage rule should apply to other legislation as well, for example, any proposal that could be shown to hurt 10 percent of the entire U.S. population seriously or for a long time. Political and judicial seminars over the meaning and measurement of serious hurt are now meeting. Whether this two stage proposal will ever become legislation is uncertain, but its very existence has already discouraged the federal government and several state governments from a few actions that could seriously hurt a sizable number of people.

No Confidence Votes

A third way of limiting presidential power was also first advocated during Gordon's presidency, inspired initially by a small band of activists and constitutional lawyers who had, years earlier, pursued ways of removing George W. Bush before the end of his second term. With insufficient support for impeachment, a stubborn president could ignore all negative feedback and stay in office even if he had lost the support of much of the country.

After bipartisan discussion, the Congress decided that the European parliamentary no confidence vote would not work in the United States. Instead, the DP suggested that when the president and the Congress cannot reach a compromise, Congress should ask the president for what the DP calls a limited no confidence vote. This vote would be restricted to White House policies that ignore congressional objections, particularly policies that the president can now initiate and implement without congressional approval. These include not only de facto war making but also signing statements that nullify a congressional vote, and significant domestic or foreign "administrative" decisions. If the president is unwilling to go along with Congress, it could request his or her resignation or propose impeachment.

Many Democrats and some Republicans and independents on Capitol Hill liked the proposal but wanted the president's support. Gordon was ambivalent about the drastic shift of power the proposal implied and urged that it be proposed as a constitutional amendment.

Federal Court Reform

Although Caruso considered a number of imaginative ways to retire some of the many conservative judges appointed by the Republicans, passionately ideological jurists with lifetime appointments are not easily dislodged. Still, the courts had to be made to accept the election results and could not continue to veto legislation the country needed and the voters had implicitly approved by electing Caruso.

During his first election campaign, Caruso had already suggested the possibility of enlarging the Supreme Court. The DP went one step further and suggested that since virtually all federal courts were now dominated by conservatives, two members be added to each to achieve some ideological balance. Otherwise too many Caruso legislative initiatives might be declared unconstitutional.

The DP hoped to start a public conversation on the subject and perhaps scare the most conservative judges into eschewing their ideological mind-set occasionally. The public conversation consisted mainly of conservative invective against the idea, however, thereby temporarily reuniting the economic and social conservatives. The polls indicated that the general public was surprisingly informed about and upset with some of the major decisions of the Supreme Court that the second Bush had solidified with his appointments, but they also showed that most people knew nothing about the lower federal courts.

Therefore, Caruso chose to ask only for the enlargement of the Supreme Court to eleven justices and to wait until he had veto proof majorities in both houses of Congress. Although the 2016 election campaign assured him of these majorities, he ultimately decided against proposing the Court's enlargement, especially since the Republicans indicated they would play the same game when they regained control of the government. Moreover, Caruso was soon able to replace enough retiring conservative judges that by 2018, liberals once again had a strong voice on the Supreme Court and many other federal courts. By the end of Gordon's first term, liberals constituted the majority in almost all of the lower federal courts. The Supreme Court turned liberal after one of its most conservative justices quit, announcing that he could not remain objective in such a hostile judicial climate.

Gordon had always thought that in the long run, the federal courts should be ideologically balanced, thereby distancing themselves from the election results and being freer to concentrate on their judicial responsibilities. The DP agreed and recommended that eventually the federal courts should be made up of equal numbers of Democrats, Republicans, and independents, at least as long as the de facto two party system remained in effect.

Following an extended national debate, some legal theorists wondered if the justices should be chosen instead by general ideological predisposition rather than by party affiliation. In the end, the question was left for the future, and now it will probably be answered by a constitutional amendment on court reform.

Toward Economic Democracy

When the DP was first organized, it briefly included a small group that called itself the radical political economy caucus and floated a bold structural change program: the creation of a second, economic U.S. Congress. It was to be called the House of Economic Representatives, and its members were to be elected to represent the economic electorate: people voting as employees (including the unemployed), employers, owners, shareholders, and other participants in the economy. (Another but outvoted part of the caucus wanted the House to be limited to employees with the others being represented by an Economic Senate.)

Almost by definition, most of the House of Economic Representatives' prospective members would be employees or employee representatives, with owners and shareholders making up a minority. In terms of power, this new body would therefore stand the economy, as well as the existing Congress, on its head, for the employees would usually be able to outvote the employers and owners.

As imagined by the DP's radical caucus, the Economic House would principally consider economic and political-economic proposals ignored or rejected by the existing Congress, but it would also introduce and debate broader issues, ranging from the nationalization of essential industries to the improvement of working conditions, freedom from computer supervision of work, and worker control, although subjects such as the levying of a wealth tax would not be ruled out.

The caucus report never saw the light of day because both the White House and the congressional leadership made it clear that publication would probably result in the DP's early demise. As might have been predicted, the report was leaked and can still be found on the Internet, although these days most of its constituency is academic and it is often excerpted in textbooks in economics and political economy.

Nonetheless, issues of economic democracy come up from time to time in Washington and in the more liberal state governments. Thus, in the mid-2020s, when the price of gasoline and the country's average summer temperature were increasing almost in tandem, a congressional committee asked the DP to determine whether and how nationalization of the oil industry could stem both sets of increases. Hernandez's Energy Secretary is reportedly ready to launch a new inquiry.

Another DP report, reputedly commissioned by Gordon's Secretary of Labor, recommended a drastic expansion of corporate boards and especially of their executive and compensation committees. The proposed additions to these committees included not only the firm's unions, worker associations, and pension fund members but also representatives from customer lobbies, those speaking for small shareholders, and the local governments in which the corporate workplaces were located.

Hernandez has already indicated that he favors the legislation and is eager to bring in owners of small, non-unionized businesses. He is also said to have a long-standing soft spot for worker control but only if other participants in the economic enterprise are not slighted. Meanwhile, the DP is toying once more with a parallel economic Congress.

WAYS OF CITIZEN EMPOWERMENT

Although the DP began its work with electoral and governmental change proposals, its staff was convinced that, in the long run, representative democracy would be strengthened most by empowering citizens to put more pressure on the people they elected to run the government. There being little of a general interest to countervail the special interests that had the most incentive to influence government, citizens with other or contradictory interests should be involved when government reached decisions.

Despite the rhetoric of citizen participation, citizens clearly could do little on their own, however, and they needed additional, even if not elected, representatives to turn their potential power into actual power. As we now know, lobbyists became the new citizen representatives, and the dramatic rise in the number of citizen lobbies may be the most significant political development of the era. Despite their many faults, these lobbies speak for the continuing albeit often prosaic interests of the unorganized citizenry.

Citizen Lobbies

Citizen lobbies that represent rank and file citizens (and some noncitizens too) in Washington and elsewhere have been active for decades. However, in 2010, the number of citizen lobbies was tiny in comparison to the number of lobbies working on behalf of corporations, formal institutions, organized professions, and the like. In terms of staff and budgets, most citizen lobbies were even smaller.

Although the line between citizen and organizational lobbies was sometimes fuzzy, even those lobbies claiming to work for citizens frequently represented formal institutions and organizations rather than ordinary citizens. Thus, there were more lobbies for school principals and teachers than for students or parents of students, more for service suppliers than for service recipients, and more for antipoverty activists than for the poor.

Three developments spurred the increase in citizen lobbies. One was the evolution of many of the social movements formed in opposition to the conservatives' virtual takeover of the country in the last quarter of the twentieth century and the beginning of this one. As the movements matured, they discovered that they were spending more and more time in lobbying. Then, when the enthusiasm and energy of their volunteer activists waned and they hired professional staffs, they realized that they were in fact becoming citizen lobbies.

For example, many women's organizations that emerged from the feminist movement have become lobbies, and so have groups favoring and fighting abortion. Initially, their lobbying often took the form of demonstrations and other protests, but now they mostly visit with elected officials to indicate where they stand, supply information, and remind the politicians of the number and kinds of citizens they speak for.

Internet political Web sites were a second source of new citizen lobbies. In fact, they already acted as such when they still existed mainly in cyberspace. Usually, the Web sites were created by experienced political activists, but sometimes bloggers with unrepresented interests discovered and joined with like-minded people. Sometimes they founded tiny social movements, and a few of these have grown large enough to become or to spin off lobbies.

The O'Hara administration was the third impetus, for when it sought to reverse legislation, close down a federal bureau, or privatize a public initiative that had flourished during the Caruso years, it frequently produced unhappy citizens who felt that their interests were being rejected. Perhaps the disappointment that followed the heady Caruso years was responsible, but more new citizen lobbies, many of them militant, appeared between 2020 and 2024 than during Caruso's two terms.

Today, there are so many lobbies that some observers believe that between elections, America is turning into a lobby democracy. Currently, for example, there are lobbies for parents and for parents of schoolchildren of various ages. Children have interests too, and several lobbies compete to speak for what they consider the best interests of the children for whom they exist.

Further lobbies represent owners of big houses and small ones, renters, and customers for everyday but expensive products and services. Lobbies for doctors, for hospitals, and for the elimination of diseases have existed since the last century, but lobbies for patients, including those suffering from specific diseases, are more recent. So are lobbies that speak for the clients of social workers and other kinds of helping professionals. The aging of the population has led to newly discovered diseases and to lobbies for those suffering from them. In addition, senior citizen lobbies have split up into lobbies representing young, middle aged, and older seniors—and the healthy older seniors are finding that their interests diverge from those of their ill age-mates.

Employees of many occupations and industries that have been unable or unwilling to unionize are served by general employee lobbies as well as by occupational or industry-wide lobbies. Employee lobbies typically search out concerned or militant workers in nonunion workplaces and industries but enroll them at home rather than in their places of employment and make fewer financial and other demands of them. Flourishing lobbies exist even for home-workers, freelancers, and the many varieties of contract and temporary workers.

After years of turf disputes and other conflicts, some unions and employee lobbies now work together on common causes. Moreover, a few lobbies have turned into unions, and some dormant unions have been revived as employee lobbies. Employee lobbies will probably never obtain the material and other resources of unions, but they are more flexible. Many unions must compromise between the interests of their active and retired workers, but retired employees can form their own lobbies that cooperate or coalesce with their old lobbies when necessary.

Most citizen lobbies, even those calling themselves membership organizations, enroll only dues payers. However, some of these individuals can be activated when lobbies need them to appear in person as a demonstration of political strength. Lobbies that cannot produce the needed members eventually have to close down. Citizen lobbies lack the economic and political clout of corporate lobbies, and if they cannot command programmed and spontaneous floods of e-mails; marching bodies; or visitors to congressional, state house, and city hall offices, they will not be effective and may not survive.

Some political philosophers are unhappy because the members of citizen lobbies rarely participate in deliberations and other forms of face-to-face democracy. Citizen lobbies, like all others, traffic in demands, money, and power, and as a result, their politics generally resemble standard interest and pressure group politics. Even so, citizen lobbies tend to be more idealistic than their corporate and organizational peers, particularly when they are still influenced by the social movements that created them.

Nevertheless, turf fights erupt as lobbies compete with each other to enroll the same citizens or fight for the same causes. Dubious recruitment methods are sometimes used to bring enough citizens to Washington to impress elected officials. Fake citizen lobbies are not unknown, nor are genuine ones that are quietly taken over by professional or trade associations with citizen names. Deceptive lobbies can be identified without too much effort, but exposing them rarely evokes much interest among the public.

Successful citizen lobbyists can earn large salaries, and those working for smaller lobbies are hired away by bigger or corporate lobbies. All known forms of cronyism, nepotism, and corruption found in other parts of the organizational world have migrated into citizen lobbying as well. Several major news media now have lobby beats, and in some years, these produce more exposés than the older political beats.

Even so, no one questions the political effectiveness of citizen lobbies. For example, the nurse-doctor program would not have passed the Congress without help from the then just organized patient lobbies. Later, parent lobbies defeated professional educator lobbies opposed to the education programs discussed in chapter 6, "Schoolings." The revised wealth tax became law during the first Gordon term in part because citizen lobbies, including major workers' lobbies, brought moderate and middle income voters to Washington to persuade their elected representatives that they really wanted a wealth tax and would vote against candidates opposing it.

Unfortunately, citizen lobbies have not yet solved their problem of "upscale democracy" (the tendency for the more affluent and educated citizenry to participate more than others and thus dominate the institutions of representative democracy). When citizen lobbies compete with each other, those with the funds to mount the greatest show of strength typically come out ahead. Also, the lobbies of the more educated and affluent citizens frequently win out over those of the less fortunate citizens.

In addition, the lobbies have probably created or at least added further to what elected officials now describe as feedback overload: being swamped with opinions, requests, demands, and the like, from citizens and groups speaking for them. Mass Conversation (which is discussed in the next section of this chapter) and other pollsters offer indirect feedback, providing information and demands that officials and politicians can ignore. However, lobby feedback, whether from corporations or citizens, is direct and not always so easily ignored unless it is clearly manufactured.

As a result, many elected officials are privately displeased by the growth of citizen lobbies, resenting the flood of requests and pressures for which they are responsible. At times, these officials complain that they are literally drowning in democracy. Admittedly, drafting legislation has become ever more difficult, and reaching decisions can occasionally take nearly forever. Indeed, at times elected officials must consider so many conflicting interests that decisions cannot be made and even compromises are out of reach.

Congress has now responded by increasing congressional staffs. All elected officials and even appointed ones who deal regularly with citizen lobbies receive help, and today, "special assistant for citizens" (assistant who interfaces with citizen lobbies) is becoming a standard Washington job description.

However, some DPers as well as public officials have suggested that a larger Congress, as much as double the size of the present one, is the most desirable solution. Smaller districts of equal size would be more representative, and the people elected to them would be more in touch with their constituents. True, such a huge assembly would be unwieldy and thus more liable to control by the leadership, but even the present-sized Congress has often been controlled by the leadership.

Mass Conversation and Polling

Mass Conversation began as a DP initiated scholarly Web site designed to elicit more information about the political activities and attitudes of rank and file Americans than could be gleaned from exit and other polls or journalistic and social science studies. The researchers wanted to engage people, especially in a sample of small towns and cities, in political conversations that would produce "thick descriptions" of their everyday political lives. Dramatic excerpts and revealing analyses would be sent to elected and appointed officials—or the staff members who do their reading for them—thereby bringing the citizenry into government in yet another way.

However, Mass Conversation never got off the ground. Only a

small number of vocal interviewees wanted to converse in this way. Subsequently, one of the site's founders ended up in Washington and established a small research center there to obtain the same information. The new Mass Conversation would obtain most of its information through polling and intensive interviewing, but it would use a conversational style and include questions usually left out or avoided by the mainstream pollsters.

The new center also had a broader purpose: to enhance communications between citizens and elected officials. Because polling sampled from the entire population, it could, in theory, reach almost everyone, but pollsters could not make people answer their questions. Consequently, Mass Conversation made special efforts to reach those who had never been near a voting booth, met an elected official, or been contacted by a pollster. By representing and perhaps even somewhat empowering the silent majority of people who remained unorganized and nonvocal, Mass Conversation hoped to supply an antidote to upscale democracy.

Although the Mass Conversation pollsters had to resort to national random sample polls to obtain legitimacy and credibility, they almost always oversampled at the lower end of the socioeconomic hierarchy. They asked only a few of the standard questions and instead got people to tell them what if anything they wanted and expected from politicians and public officials. The interviewers encouraged people to talk about subjects they discussed with family and friends or had kept to themselves, and they carefully gauged the intensity of people's feelings about the topics that came up.

Later, the informal talks evolved into more formal, occasionally lengthy interviews and a more rigorous form of the conversations the original organization had sought. Today, Washington sees the interviews as rich data about what people want and what they expect from government. These interviews have become an equivalent of the backyard and cracker barrel conversations politicians believe citizens once held in an earlier America.

Unfortunately, Mass Conversation lacks a secure political base and therefore has been a convenient target for individuals and groups inside and outside the government who think that in an interdependent world beset with increasingly complex problems, politics should be left to the politically educated. Consequently, they oppose Mass Conversation's concern for the politically uneducated and its eagerness to talk to nonvoters. They are especially upset by the interviews with the so-called impulsives: citizens, who react randomly and impulsively, often on the basis of false or imagined information—even though these can sometimes become last minute swing voters in close elections.

Adult Political Education

After Hernandez introduced political education courses for the country's schools, the DP developed adult versions for all available educational venues, for political clubs and party training programs, and even for the undergraduate political science departments that saw political education as an intrinsic part of the liberal arts. However, those student bodies were either small or had already educated themselves politically. The adults who wanted nothing further to do with schooling were harder to reach and had little interest in classes that lacked occupational payoffs or entertainment value. And the DP did not have the money and expertise to launch a new adult education venture.

The DP decided to rely on the mass media instead. It sought advice from dramatists and other writers as well as artists, composers, and media-using educators. Television and Internet dramas for teens and young adults borrowed some ideas from successful student political courses and exercises, presenting stories in which people studied the politics of their workplaces and other local organizations. Few attracted a significant audience, although the DP programmers fared better when they commissioned some novelists writing for the romance and adventure markets.

Reality TV and Internet programs had contestants running against each other for simulated local political offices and subsequently for national offices as well, including the White House. The DP and its advisers came up with a few somewhat original programs that attracted respectable audiences. *Compromise* asked contestants for solutions to a variety of mostly local political impasses, to persuade political factions to agree on a single candidate, or to resolve disputes over a municipal budget.

However, the most popular program was *Family Politics,* a saga about a highly politicized family in which the several generations argued about a variety of political matters. The series ran long enough to include installments about necessary wars, income redistribution, the pros and cons of constitutional amendments, and married couples running together for president and vice president.

Politicians developed a fondness for updated remakes of old political movies and TV series after their producers decided to place politicians in cameos and then even in minor starring roles. Eventually, a giant media conglomerate proposed a set of series in which actual candidates for high elective office could show how they would make decisions if elected. When the White House and the Congress let it be known that such a venture would erase the already thin line between politics and entertainment, the potential sponsors decided to bow out, although many observers of electoral politics still like the idea behind the series.

The DP was most pleased by a documentary vaguely modeled on an old newspaper column called "Action Line" in which people with real complaints against public agencies and business firms were helped to seek correction or restitution. The dramatization of actual events allows the writers to include some lessons about bureaucratic and political processes as well. Unlike the outcomes reported in the old newspaper columns, many of the episodes end in failure, allowing the writers to explain the variety of decision-making criteria used by public and private bureaucracies.

The DP harbored no illusions about its educational achievements. Because they have been given little opportunity—and even less incentive—to participate in the political process, adults have seen little need for educating themselves politically. However, the DP is hoping that what the youngsters now participating in political education courses and projects are learning will stay with them when they become adults. Some educators believe that if the workweek really declines below twenty-five hours, some people will want to use their extra hours for further schooling, including in politics.

The *Weekly Democrat*

The DP's media ambitions extended beyond political education; in fact it wanted to start an alternative news medium, which it originally described as a citizen newspaper but that ended up as a multi-media venture. The project called the *Weekly Democrat* was, however, staffed largely by citizens, more specifically by citizen journalists, people with sufficient training or experience to gather news under professional supervision. Most had been editors of their college papers or the masters of student news Web sites. A handful of professional journalists who edited and produced the Web site/program/magazine, and sometimes assigned stories, provided the supervision.

The *Democrat* saw its mandate as complementing the establishment perspective and elite cum middle class bias of the mainstream news media. Consequently, the citizen journalists reported events from locations and in sectors of society rarely visited by mainstream journalists. Sometimes, they came upon and exposed instances of private and public corruption or incompetence in unexpected places. More often, they corrected stories coming out of the mainstream news media.

For example, the Washington reporters for the *Democrat*, once they were admitted to White House press conferences and had made contacts in all the federal agencies, were able to ask questions, even of the president, that the mainstream journalists could not ask so readily or did not think to ask. Of course, the White House and federal agency heads objected if the *Democrat*'s journalists became too inquisitive, and some lasted only a few months before no one called on them anymore and they had to be replaced.

Although the *Democrat* described itself as nonpartisan, its mandate, the journalists it attracted, and the stories it published rarely pleased the Republicans and other conservatives. It also displeased liberals in government, especially at the executive level, who had been co-opted by or had to defend their agencies.

Today the *Weekly Democrat*'s distinctive approach has enabled it to attract enough audience, ads, and foundation grants to split off from the DP and become independent. It pays union scale salaries, which allow the best citizen journalists to become full-time staffers, and bureaus have been established in major cities around the country.

Once the *Democrat* had been launched, the DP began to develop or inspire special news services, syndicated columns, and Web sites, some of which existed only temporarily and some that have become permanent—a few of them in mainstream electronic and digital media. *Citizens,* the initial site, covers the doings of citizen (and other) lobbies, and most of its stories wind up in the *Weekly Democrat* and other alternative news media.

Rumor, which began as a popular Internet site and is now a regular news service, verifies or debunks the rumors that, thanks to imaginative bloggers and their sources, regularly travel up and down the country. The service specializes in quashing rumors about terrorist incidents, climatic disasters, and serial murders that can easily evoke fear and panic.

Exposé explores extended results of investigative reporting schemes, especially the follow-ups that report corrections made or not made after the exposés appeared. For example, when investigative reporters identify the responsible "villains," the follow-ups look into how and why the villains were successful and what structural changes if any are made to prevent new villains from emerging after the exposés have been forgotten.

Investigative journalism is very expensive, and most of its stories have to be sold as exclusives to one of the mainstream news media, which use them to scoop their rivals. The *Democrat* usually picks up the follow-ups, which are not exciting enough to attract the mainstream audience.

Some of the DP's inventions lasted only briefly. One notable early failure, *Analysis,* featured a rotating array of public intellectuals offering analyses of the week's major news that went beyond those originating with journalists, columnists, and op-ed authors. The program demanded too much instant analytic originality from the public intellectuals and too much sophistication and dedication from its audiences.

A related format, *Ideology,* analyzed the ideological assumptions and frames of the various participants in headline making events. The analysis was used to identify the major ideologies at work in the United States and abroad, to acquaint mainstream America with the workings of ideology, and in the process to lay bare the ideologies of the mainstream itself. *Ideology* did not make it on television and as a newspaper column, but it has survived on the Internet and is assigned in a variety of college courses. When it expanded its operations to look also at the ideologies of the journalists covering these events, *Ideology* was adopted in journalism courses.

Another flop was *Squabbling,* which looked more deeply into disagreements, mostly at publicly reported congressional and state legislature hearings and committee meetings. Because many Americans dismiss or attack these as squabbling, every program featured a citizens' panel who identified the squabbling, indicated why it was unnecessary, and offered what they considered obvious solutions. Then, the officials who had participated in the alleged squabbles came on to explain the value, interest, and constituency differences that led to their disagreements and evaluated the solutions coming from the citizens' panel.

The program was both too complicated for a nonpolitical audience and too repetitious. It lasted only a few weeks, and the DP educators are trying to come up with another way of teaching that disagreement is endemic to a democracy and a single solution that satisfies everyone can be found only rarely.

THE DARK SIDE OF DEMOCRACY

Despite all its efforts, the DP has so far not made much progress in what Project people call lighting up the dark side of democracy. The dark side includes not only upscale democracy, habitual nonvoting, and related distancing from the polity but also a range of antidemocratic behaviors and feelings.

The DP worries most about people who consistently want a strong leader, and some of its electoral and other reforms are intended to prevent political crises in which demand for such a leader can increase and spread. However, the economy and the rest of the world, including unpredictable weather, can quickly create such crises. Some people now think that 9/11 prevented people from seeing that the call for a unitary executive during the Bush years could lead to the beginnings of dictatorship. This is why the DP has been so insistent on increasing the power of the Congress over the executive.

Even so, the White House continues to be the primary political institution and the one with readiest and fastest access to the guns that remain the ultimate levers of power. More to the point, the White House can still start or at least stoke a war fever that starts elsewhere—and even a powerful Congress is not immune to catching that fever. Some DP staffers believe that the Supreme Court ought to be given the exclusive power to make the decision to go to war.

The DP is concerned as well with the impulsives. As mentioned earlier in this chapter, the impulsives are people who become politically active rarely and unexpectedly but then act impulsively. Such individuals are also most likely to catch and pass on war fever.

Although impulsiveness has many causes, it often accompanies anger, and such anger has often unduly shaped American politics. Older heads remember the anger of social, religious, and economic conservatives, as well as of radical and liberal antiwar groups and young people with a variety of grievances. Some DPers are finally trying to figure out how to respond intelligently to outbreaks of national anger and to eliminate the conditions that generate the anger. Even now, both the White House and Congress pay special attention to situations and conditions that generate intense anger.

AMENDING THE CONSTITUTION

Early in his second term, Caruso had already suggested, albeit tentatively, that it was time to rethink or amend the Constitution. His trial balloon aroused instant support from the liberals and the Left, approval from many centrists, opposition from the Right, and the organization of a new libertarian movement whose members wondered whether the country even needed a constitution.

Caruso never returned to the idea publicly, but the DP started thinking about how to update the Constitution. The O'Hara administration kept the DP so busy defending the electoral and structural improvements made during the Caruso years that the Constitution update was put on a back burner.

Gordon, however, encouraged the DP to resume its activity and used the 2026 State of the Union speech to urge the country to think about whether it wanted the present Constitution, an amended one, or a brand new one. For the next several years, lectures, meetings, conferences, and even mock constitutional conventions were held all over the country to debate this question as well as to draft new constitutions and amendments to the existing one. The pollsters and elected officials with their ears on the ground of their districts reported that only a tiny number wanted a new constitution, that a plurality was satisfied with the present one, but that a somewhat larger plurality was prepared to accept an amended document. Many people were of course unfamiliar with all but a few of the Constitution's articles.

Gordon then set up a constitutional office in the White House that reviewed the hundreds of amendments that had been proposed over the years and proposed a long list of about twenty possible amendments. After the 2030 midterm elections, which increased the liberal majorities in both houses of Congress, Gordon was ready to take the next step. Discussions with congressional leaders, officials from the major and some minor parties, governors from various parts of the country, and experts in constitutional law persuaded her to propose six amendments, leaving the Congress to decide whether it would pass fewer or add further amendments.

Using several addresses to the nation, Gordon explained that the health of representative democracy and today's national and international problems required updating the Constitution. She then announced the White House list of amendments and suggested that Congress as well as the state legislatures take the necessary next steps.

Gordon had hoped that the Congress would approve the amendments before she left office, but as she had feared, her short list was criticized by every group whose favorite amendments had been left out. Before long, Congress had more than doubled the number of amendments, and the public discussion segued into the 2032 election, some of which was devoted to debating which amendments should move forward. The president plays no formal role in the process of amending the Constitution, but not long after Hernandez moved into the Oval Office, the congressional leadership announced the six amendments it favored. None were very different from those already suggested by Gordon.

The amendments can be summarized as follows.

1. One Person One Vote. *Every person eligible to vote is entitled to one duly recorded vote in all governmental elections. In addition, all federal elected officials must represent a roughly equal number of people, and the organizations and other bodies in which they operate must be restructured accordingly if necessary to reflect this principle.*

This amendment corrects the failure of the Founding Fathers to state unequivocally that all citizens have the right to vote, and it enters the one person one vote principle into the Constitution. By implication, it also calls for fractional voting in the Senate. In addition, it can be interpreted to invalidate winner-take-all votes in primaries as well as in congressional and presidential elections and in the Electoral College. As a result, there is actually no need to abolish the Electoral College. The amendment's reference to a duly recorded vote seeks to prevent voting irregularities and requires that all votes be counted before an election can be certified.

The amendment as written is politically difficult to reject. However, both parties know that once presidents are elected by a majority of the popular vote, Democrats have a better chance to end up in the Oval Office, at least as long as so many big states and big cities vote overwhelmingly Democratic. Thus, the Republicans must figure out how they can block the amendment without appearing to oppose majoritarian democracy.

The amendment entails some additional significant consequences. According to Article V of the Constitution, which describes requirements for amending the Constitution, "no state, without its consent, shall be deprived of its equal suffrage in the Senate." This sentence appears to bar any attempt to reduce the number of senators allotted to each state. However, it does not explicitly forbid fractionalizing the votes of these senators according to each state's proportion of the country's total population. Depending on the final language of this amendment, should it survive, the Supreme Court might have to decide whether fractional voting constitutes "equal suffrage" or whether the phrase itself could be redefined so as to embrace fractional votes.

2. Money is not Speech. *Freedom of speech does not include the spending of money to disseminate that speech.*

The amendment is intended to invalidate *Buckley v. Valeo* and other Court decisions that prohibit caps on spending for campaign advertising, whatever the form of the ads. Most likely, the final draft of the amendment will define free speech and limit it explicitly to the direct expression of ideas so as to separate expression from dissemination.

Some legal observers believe that the one person one vote amendment could eventually reform present campaign funding practices to preempt the need for this amendment, especially if the courts accept the argument that donors who contribute more than a nominal sum effectively now have more than one vote.

3. Court Realignment. *The Supreme Court is to consist of three judges who declare themselves Democrats, three Republicans, and three who declare themselves independent. Other federal courts shall be apportioned in an equivalent manner.*

The drafters hope that this amendment, originally suggested by the DP, would minimize the possibility that a party that dominates the other two branches of government and fills the courts with its adherents could thereby maintain at least some of its power for many years after it has left office. The amendment thus maintains the checks and balances system, making the courts more independent of election results and requiring them to put greater emphasis on judicial considerations.

Some people still argue that the checks and balances aim would be better achieved by naming equal proportions of conservatives, liberals, and centrists. Radicals belong on this list as well, but an amendment placing radicals in the courts will not fly politically right now.

A number of lawyers and law professors are organizing to propose a substitute amendment with the same general purpose. It would abolish lifetime appointments to the Supreme Court, replacing them with staggered eighteen-year terms as suggested by the legal theorist Sanford Levinson. Then, all future presidents would be able to name two new justices during each four-year term. Others are suggesting that the same principle be applied to all federal courts.

4. No Confidence Vote. *The Congress can, with the agreement of two-thirds of its members, vote no confidence in specific presidential decisions or policies. The president can thereafter alter the deci-*

sions or policies in question or resign the office, in which case the vice president serves the remainder of the president's term.

The Congress shall also have the right, by the same vote, to recall any elected or appointed official from all three branches of the federal government for documented malfeasance and incompetence.

Hernandez, like Gordon before him, favors parliamentary government and proportional representation, but both know that the Congress would never approve either change. They therefore went along with another DP idea, which would prevent presidents from making clearly disastrous decisions or initiating harmful long term policies that Congress cannot overrule, and that could therefore hurt and even endanger the country until the next presidential election or longer.

Some worst case analysts worry that a stampeded or panicked Congress could saddle the country with unacceptable policies that a wise president could prevent. White House advisers believe this part of the amendment could severely inhibit the president. They hope that the amendment will either be completely rethought or quietly withdrawn.

The second part of the amendment is a supplement to the impeachment article and is designed to increase the power of Congress to remove the president and other federal officials. It still requires agreed upon definitions of malfeasance and incompetence.

Opponents of unnecessary wars want malfeasance to include some reference to unacceptable war making and killing of civilians. The environmental lobbies that are worried about climate change want malfeasance defined so broadly as to include the unnecessary loss of life and limb resulting from natural disasters.

5. Equal Rights. *All legislation creating equal rights must include provisions for attaining equal outcomes as quickly as possible.*

This amendment responds to insistent demands for putting teeth into racial, gender, religious, privacy, and other rights legislation. The Congress is unlikely to approve it until implications across all rights have been considered, more specifics are added about the attainment of equal outcomes, and the government is protected if equal outcomes cannot be achieved. Most constitutional lawyers believe this amendment can only be approved in emasculated form.

> 6. Full Employment. *Everyone seeking employment is entitled to full-time work at no less than a living wage or salary that is indexed to the median wage or salary.*

Like his Democratic predecessors, Hernandez believes strongly in full employment, and he thinks the amendment could be approved if *full time* is left undefined, because *full time* might one day mean a thirty or even twenty-five hour workweek This amendment would require equal access to full-time jobs for everyone. Moreover, the amendment redefines the living wage as a proportion of the median wage.

Critics of this amendment argue that only the government can implement it, thereby giving the government immense power over the economy. Supporters believe that the amendment could be implemented by creating sufficient Community Service Work Program jobs.

Rewriting the Preamble

The drafters also proposed a revision of the Constitution's preamble, treating it as an additional amendment to the Constitution. They did not, however, supply a formal draft of the new preamble. Instead, they recommended that a new preamble borrow the opening of the Declaration of Independence, stating that all human beings are created equal but adding that human beings are therefore entitled to establish a society in which they can live as equals. The drafters also urged a sentence to the effect that all human beings are created to be free to pursue their own happiness provided that they do not interfere with the happiness of others. This freedom should acknowledge the right of all human beings to control their own minds and bodies.

The first part of the preamble was inserted in case the equal rights amendment did not survive. The freedom provision acknowledged the conservative and libertarian demands for a statement to this effect. The reference to minds and bodies will, it is hoped, turn advocates of privacy rights, defenders of women's choice, and those still hoping for eventual recognition of the fetus into supporters of the amendments. It can also be interpreted to put limits on genetic engineering.

Some advocates for the freedom provision would prefer to include it in an additional amendment, arguing that it will significantly expand the constituency of the Bill of Rights. At present, the Bill mainly affects journalists, academics, writers, artists, and related "creative" occupations but is rarely relevant to everyday speech or to the speech-related freedoms of ordinary people.

Actually, most who worked on the preamble hoped the entire statement would become a possible seventh amendment. However, both Hernandez and the congressional Democratic leadership felt its egalitarian sentiment would enrage economic conservatives. They would welcome a popular demand, preferably of tidal wave proportion, to add it to the present preamble of the Constitution and turn the revised preamble into the initial article of the amended Constitution.

Passing the Amendments

The White House is now debating when to begin the process of obtaining approval for the six amendments and the preamble from the Congress and the state legislatures. Hernandez has talked them over with congressional leaders as well as the governors and legislative leaders of enough of the fifty states to be upbeat. The general public's support seems sufficiently solid too. Nonetheless, other amendments could be introduced in the Congress, notably by religious and other outlier groups whose ideas have been ignored. However, the state legislatures cannot reasonably be expected to agree on a large number of diverse amendments, and even six may be too many.

Meanwhile, some of the DP's populists are already thinking about how to make it possible, someday, to amend the Constitution by popular vote.

CHAPTER EIGHT

2033 AND BEYOND

By the summer of 2033, Hernandez knew that much of his time and energy would be taken up with the ongoing attempt to amend the Constitution. He had sensed that the country, or at least his supporters in the electorate, wanted a period of political quiet, with only the most urgently needed new legislation and as few political battles as possible. Accordingly, Hernandez campaigned primarily on his reputation as a policy wonk and proposed to improve on the programs that Caruso and Gordon had initiated.

Both Caruso and Gordon had left Hernandez an ever more expensive set of responsibilities. For example, the small classes teaching program instituted by the Small Class Initiative has now spread across the entire country but still requires new expenditures for classroom construction and teacher training. Another costly item is the universal Medicare program, which will probably never stop growing. At the moment, the last post–World War II baby boomers are in their seventies and many will eventually need costly care. The nurse-doctor program has been so successful that it has raised everyone's health expectations, and even young people now have medical examinations when they feel ill. Funds for these and other innovations must come in part from the still novel tax reforms of the last decade, some of which remain under attack.

Being careful and wanting to plan ahead, Hernandez asked his Council of Long-Range Advisers for a report on the most urgent problems likely to face the nation in the 2030s and even beyond. The report would help him and Vice President Shirley Johnson understand their constraints and get a better sense of their legislative options.

The essence of the Council's report follows.

THE ECONOMY

The Council hopes that a number of new economic growth innovations to spur economic growth will soon appear, for example, postcomputer and postdigital technologies to replace the present ones, some of which date from the last century. Without these or other new sources of economic growth, the country must probably look forward to more of the present pattern: slow growth, especially in number of jobs and wages, during good economic times and contraction during bad times. All other things being equal, more jobs will disappear during the bad times, and fewer will return when the economy recovers.

However, the ups and downs may come faster than they have in the past, requiring the government also to find faster ways of reacting. Perhaps the Federal Reserve needs to meet monthly to change interest rates, or perhaps quick income fixes like President Caruso's may be in order. Further tax increases, if necessary, should be levied on multicontinental and multinational corporations that operate in the United States. Those corporations not paying their fair share for the public services they use or the externalities they create should be tapped first. Someday, a future United Nations will need to levy an international tax on all such firms that evade their responsibilities to the nations in which they do business.

Preserving full-time jobs and creating further jobs in the United States is a continuing challenge. However, some manufacturing, assembly, and service jobs that were outsourced during the past two decades could be brought back as overseas wages for unskilled and semiskilled work continue to increase, coming closer to lower level American wages. The United States cannot compete with subminimal wage paying regions and nations, but American workers can make up for their still higher pay by being more productive than foreign workers.

During economic downturns, the total number of workers will exceed the number of needed work hours. To prevent mass layoffs, the federal government must see to it that employers, especially large ones—and their workers—share the available work instead. The Community Service Work Program that was begun experimentally under Gordon (see chap. 2, "Healing the Economy") will probably have to become a regular federal responsibility.

In regions in which the average workweek has fallen below thirty hours, the federal government should be ready to supply at least five weekly hours of public work for those needing further income from work. When and where the average workweek declines to twenty-five hours, the government ought to offer ten or more weekly hours. The cost of the program will be significant, but it offers a productive way of improving public works and public services while stabilizing the economy.

Local and state governments must draw up plans for using the part-time workers. The interests of full-time workers will have to be protected to prevent politically costly conflict with the part-timers. Although the latter's job preferences need to be taken into account, the part-timers will be among the lowest ranked employees in the organizations that they will serve, and they will have to accept that status.

Global Warming, Energy Austerity, and Cultural Pain

Now that world scientists and the leaders of most countries, including the United States, finally agree that global warming will be a serious problem for the foreseeable future, the Council suggests a change in American policy. The United States, together with Europe, should temporarily contribute a greater share of the world's needed reduction of dangerous emissions. In exchange, the nations that are not meeting their assigned emission removal quota would have to offer trade, investment, and related concessions that can spur employment and economic growth in America and Europe. Small third world nations can continue to be free riders if they make at least a nominal effort to reduce emissions.

Despite the two decades long experience in developing alternative energy sources, the major current sources, from biomass to solar panels and wind farms, will never be as efficient or inexpensive as the fossil fuels that most increase global warming. The government should continue to develop alternative sources for coal and oil, especially those that ciptizens can supply on their own. However, until cheap, nonpolluting, and "green" battery technology is available, the political and economic pressures to continue to rely on coal and oil may be insurmountable.

Actually, the perfection of a quickly rechargeable and replaceable and totally "green" plug-in car battery should have the highest priority. If it can be mass-produced, Americans will finally accept tiny cars and take impossible burdens off mass transit.

Moreover, all energy prices will doubtless continue to rise, hurting those who can least afford the price rise the most severely. The government may then be under intense pressure to subsidize energy prices. The wiser, if politically more difficult, solution is to ration energy, at least minimally.

Given the country's diversity, the rationing itself might best be left to individual states provided they meet federal guidelines. However, even a minimal rationing program will impress the country that energy usage has to decline.

Meanwhile, mass transit must be made available virtually everywhere, even if in many places the vehicle is a van or a jitney. In the long run, everyone except in isolated and lightly developed parts of the country should count on walking or bicycling access to a transit stop. The construction of transitways on expressway lanes in the larger metropolitan areas must be accelerated.

All of the Council's projections indicate that energy prices, and therefore most other prices, will continue to increase and may never come down again. If total work hours shrink at the same time and wage and salary levels do not rise, most people will face declines in purchasing power. In that case, they will have to alter their standard of living, giving up some goods and services that they have come to define as necessities.

Although the Council believes that Americans are neither as materialistic nor as obsessed with shopping as cultural critics insist, the country will face a period of austerity, the consequences of which cannot yet be predicted. On the one hand, most Americans have learned to adapt to austerity before. They have put off purchases and have lived with rationing but usually as a means to national survival, especially in major depressions and in world wars. In both cases, austerity has been widely shared, at least in the working and middle classes.

However, the country as a whole has not had to cut back significantly on consumption for a long time, and some national cultural and psychological problems could develop. The Council expects the arrival of cultural pain, which could be felt as a national malaise or as downward mobility.

Downward mobility that is not widely shared could bring about public anger, as well as authoritarian social movements, and the identification of new scapegoats that can be blamed for a decline in the American way of life. Conversely, some people will take a shrinking standard of living out on themselves, through depression and the other social pathologies that often accompany downward mobility.

Consequently, if cutbacks in the standard of living become necessary, the government must be able to show that they are borne by everyone. Although the wealth tax should eventually reduce extreme economic inequalities and the accompanying excesses in conspicuous consumption, the government can levy emergency luxury taxes to further discourage the latter. Still, it is also possible that, within limits, people may enjoy the conspicuous consumption of others, especially celebrities who are only briefly conspicuous.

Government cannot cure cultural pain, but it may be asked to lessen the monetary pains of lifestyle reductions. It ought to start thinking about how these pains could be lessened and the economy helped at the same time. One long-term possibility is a basic or citizens' income: a monthly or quarterly stipend to which every citizen or resident is entitled by virtue of being a member of society.

The idea is hardly new, and although it would be automatically taxed away from affluent Americans, a wholesale reorganization of the country's public finance structure would be required. A temporary basic income might be considered if the future were to bring such sharp reductions in work and work time that in some years large numbers of people no longer earn enough to pay the bills.

Under such conditions, the government would also be under pressure to undertake deprivatization, creating public services to replace private ones people can no longer afford. Deprivatization would be hard on an already overburdened federal budget and would of course be fought by the businesses that would be hurt directly, by the larger business community, and by the ideological defenders of laissez-faire.

Over the last quarter century, many Americans have learned that sometimes and for specific functions and activities, government is more effective and efficient than private enterprise. The western European countries learned this lesson in the last century and, thanks in part to the bridging work of labor parties, long ago achieved a generally workable division of labor between government and business. But in America, old beliefs and economic power structures die hard.

Years ago, President Caruso suggested another approach: that private enterprise and government should compete, letting the customers choose the winner. His suggestion was never fully tried, but it might be given a chance as well if and when the economic conditions require a drastic structural and cultural change.

WAR AND PEACE

Global warming and energy austerity can be expected to cause new international tensions. The still increasing competition for oil—and even for land for biomass and wind farms—is likely to complicate further relations between the competing nations. Wherever the earth is affected by energy shortages and the effects of global warming, struggles for the control of vital resources will escalate, increasing the danger of new wars. Alliances between nations supplying energy and those buying it could encourage new economic wars, resulting in other ways of killing and wounding their victims. More peacekeepers will be needed, and eventually new peacemaking responsibilities may be forced on the United Nations.

No one who has read the twentieth-century novel *1984* can forget George Orwell's image of the world's being divided between two continent sized tyrannical superpowers, often taken to be the United States and China, locked in permanent war. But Orwell was wrong: the competition for oil alone involves more than two giants. Yet other competitions suggest that the world may eventually be structured in continental or semicontinental unions of states following the lead set long ago by the European Union. America should encourage such unions, in part because they can function as countervailing influences against superpowers.

Of course, unions of the sort just described would require the United States to give up what remains of its superpower status, but for two decades now, the White House has worked toward this goal, as well as to end the manifest or latent pursuit of an American empire. To be sure, a desperate America could resume its march toward empirehood, for example by seeking control over a large proportion of the world's oil or the land areas most suitable for biomass farming. Moreover, China could do the same, and then Orwell might be proved right after all. However, if the current political climate in both countries and across the world persists, wars to create empires will not take place.

Orwell may have been wrong in another way. The various international competitions will likely be fought out not only by states and continental unions of states but by multicontinental and multinational corporations, including those that control the various sources of both fossil fuels and alternative energy. Wars between giant corporations are unlikely, but wars between nation-states pressured or egged on by such corporations are always possible.

The energy and global warming competitions do, however, provide an opportunity for nation-states and unions of states to test methods of controlling or regulating the intercontinental and international business firms. If enough international employee unions of sufficient size emerge, they would add an additional countervailing element to the competition.

Civil Wars and Terrorism

Now that the popular opposition to unnecessary wars has spread over the globe and is being taken seriously by most governments, warlike behavior is most likely to break out in civil wars or in highly polarized countries on the verge of civil war. As earlier in the century, these usually involve numerically superior but politically and economically inferior populations. The conflict may, however, be perceived as one between ethnic, racial, religious, or other populations.

The Council urges that the United States continue to join in UN sponsored attempts to prevent such civil wars before they start, if necessary even by induced regime change. Further, when the opportunity can be made available, contending populations ought to be tempted with emigration to other countries. Population decanting can sometimes reduce population and other pressures that lead to or continue civil wars, and it may cut down on the number of refugees. Whenever possible, the United States ought to use international organizations that it can influence to reduce economic imbalances between competing populations.

Civil wars and other internal disputes can be expected to produce further attacks on innocent civilians, and these attacks will still probably be defined as terrorism. The national and international intelligence operations and the rapid strike forces, American, foreign, and UN, are by now sophisticated enough to prevent most sizable attacks. Still, suicide bombers and the international equivalents of roadside bombs can be brought into any country.

Suitcase size nuclear weapons are not out of the question, although the same mutual assured destruction (MAD) constraints that avoided nuclear war during the twentieth-century cold war period can be brought into play again. Even the most militant insurgent groups can be made to realize that if they or their associates resort to nuclear terrorism, their own communities and regions will be struck in return. Pinpoint bombing is now accurate enough to target the required revenge.

Although the third world has shrunk now that every country is industrialized and modernized enough to supply inexpensive goods and low wage labor to the world economy, it will likely remain the major source of both civil wars and exported terrorism. Indeed, a revolution of rising democratic expectations may set off more such wars, especially where unrepresentative elites remain in control.

If the United States can avoid becoming involved in these conflicts, insurgents, including violent ones who might otherwise violate or invade our shores, or those of other countries, may limit themselves to fighting with national or regional enemies, and civil wars can be contained. By now the international community has had more than enough practice in doing so, although the United Nations must still learn to step in before civil wars become genocidal.

Eventually, the United Nations must also be prepared for the possibility that it will someday have to become a world authority. For the moment, few nations are ready to accept it as such an authority, but if dramatic climatic changes, conflicts over oil, and other pervasive world crises develop, a world authority may become so necessary that it finally will have to be invented.

THE DOMESTIC POLITY

If all six or most of the constitutional amendments pass during the years Hernandez is in the White House, both the country and the president should benefit from the national "high" likely to follow. Congress will probably follow up with legislation to implement the amendments, but the courts will have to have their say about the new legislation. Thus, immediate political and governmental change should not be expected.

If the one person one vote amendment is passed and the courts eventually end the excessive power of the small states, the biggest states and their populations will be the political winners. All other things being equal, the country will be more democratic, in both senses of the word. In fact, the Democratic majority, and the size of its liberal wing, should increase. If that majority supplies good governance, the party could even look forward, for better or worse, to many years of political dominance.

The Council is nonpartisan and cannot take political sides, but someone will need to remind the Democratic party of the dangerous precedents set by the Bush administration at the start of the century to create a long-term one party state. However, the Democrats must also remember that either long-term power still finally corrupts too much of the governing party or the voters get tired of the same faces and decide to give the opposing party another chance.

But if the decline in voter party loyalty and the increase in the number of independent voters continue, the Democrats may never obtain that majority. We should not soon expect a three party polity, but election campaigns in which both parties must compete for old and new blocs of independent voters will throw up new issues, require new ways of campaigning, and bring new uncertainties to election outcomes. Someday, an ad hoc independent party will likely send its candidate to the Oval Office.

Conversely, the passage of the amendments to the Constitution could create some negative side effects for the Hernandez administration. For one thing, they could generate a conservative backlash, including a remobilization of some conservative social movements and think tanks, although only if these can produce credible rhetoric. Groups promoting amendments that were not considered in the first round may ask for another round of amending the Constitution.

Another possible side effect is a further growth of upscale democracy, which is likely to become more serious as citizen influence grows. No amendments or laws can stop the more affluent and educated from continuing to vote more often and from mobilizing more quickly than less fortunate citizens. The upscale citizens can communicate more effectively with their elected representatives, and they play the largest role in the citizen—and other—lobbies. The government and the courts must protect the one person one vote principle at both the de jure and de facto levels, and Democrats must remember and reassert Caruso's concern for the below median income population.

The corporate equivalent of upscale democracy is the co-optation of regulators by the regulated. The White House and Congress must watch the major regulatory agencies carefully, just as they must discourage the Internal Revenue Service from tolerating the tax evading strategies of wealthier constituents. However, the citizen lobbies must watch the government at the same time.

Yet the government also needs to keep an eye on the lobbies. Some citizen lobbies have by now copied all the undesirable, harmful, and corrupt practices previously associated with business and professional lobbies. In addition, the lobbies representing more economically or politically powerful citizens have taken undue advantage of weaker citizens.

Fairness and Equality

Despite the egalitarian policies of past administrations, opposition to these policies remains a recurring challenge. Moreover, trends countering these policies develop even in the fairest societies. For example, if economic growth depends on highly skilled and thus full-time well paid workers and the wages of the less skilled remain static, economic inequality must increase. Layoffs, declines in the workweek, and other effects of economic slowdowns produce the same result. The Community Service Work Program could therefore become a major player in the maintenance of economic fairness.

Short of the revival of comprehensive affirmative action and the institution of equally comprehensive reparations policies oriented to present generations, progress toward racial equality will be slow. Every new wave of immigration may increase the vulnerability of the remaining African Americans and other dark skinned Americans who are included in the racialized lowest income class rightly called America's undercaste. Conversely, economic growth and the likely growth in the size of government will offer additional opportunities for poor racial minorities to enter into or to anchor themselves in the middle class.

The concurrent increase in racial and ethnic intermarriage and the growing number of multiracial Americans should begin to have a positive effect on racial equality. Intermarriage will also "deracialize" the Latino population, which might finally end white fears of the Latinization of American society. Even so, white fears about becoming a minority will not disappear, and nativists can be expected to look for ways to increase the white population. The White House may be under pressure to provide asylum to white immigrants from foreign countries that are not trouble spots.

Although economically driven immigration may slow down when the economy is in a downward mode, in better times the probationary immigration system [described in chap. 4, "Fighting for Fairness"] may sometimes be overwhelmed by so many new arrivals that the category of illegal immigrant will reappear. Moreover, if foreign policy needs, especially for population decanting in countries engaged in civil wars, require the United States to admit more people from such countries, overall immigration policy may have to be rethought.

The Hernandez administration would be well advised to keep an eye on gender equality trends. If a slow economy hastens the downward economic slide of males, the government will have to figure out what if anything it can do to reduce the slide and the pain it induces. The administration will also have to consider the political and cultural reverberations that are likely to follow.

Populations that have been used to dominating their societies often take the loss of power hard, and their anger could produce revenge seeking and other harmful reactions. In earlier societies, men could be sent off to hunts or wars to recoup some status. In our time, government could try affirmative action programs for men, although these may have to run concurrently with other programs that tackle the remaining labor market and other inequalities for women. Gender politics could become very complicated.

Family, Home, and Community Issues

The Council can predict with some assurance that the continuing rise in childless families and singles households will eventually result in a noticeable reduction in the number of children born to nonimmigrant Americans. As long as immigration continues, the country will have a sufficient number of children, and even poor immigrants may be valued because of the children they bring with them or produce once in America.

The periodic loneliness and depression that now still accompany singlehood can cast shadows across the larger society, even though there will soon be enough different kinds of singles that one term for them will no longer suffice. As their number increases, compensatory cultural and institutional responses may be invented. In the meantime, the Gordon administration's demon-chasing program will have to be tested and then developed further.

The Council has nothing new to say about home and community issues, the Caruso and Gordon administrations having already considered most of the long-term problems and possibilities. [See chap. 5, "Family, Home, and Community."] Should energy costs decline and global warming slow down, the country may not have to alter its driving habits or move out of the single family house as quickly and completely as once thought. Conversely, if both trends speed up, the incumbent administration and the economic leadership will each be biting several political bullets concurrently.

Whatever happens, the plan to consolidate the country's landmass by shutting down nearly empty or unlivable areas is moving ahead slowly. The younger generations are not absorbing the traditional nostalgia for idealized small town and rural America, and the cost of fuel has put the weekend house, often located in declining areas, out of reach of all but very rich Americans.

Schooling for the New Economy

Now that small classes are the norm in public education, new educational policy should take two directions. One is to make sure that the teachers staffing the small classes are themselves as well trained as possible, not only in their subjects and teaching techniques but also in their ability to understand the changing society in which they are workers. Many teachers complement the curriculum they teach with the conventional wisdoms they have learned in their everyday lives. As a result, teachers have frequently been, unintentionally, among the more effective transmitters of outdated myths, inaccurate stereotypes and misinformation. When the stereotypes are racist, teachers are often publicly corrected and chastised, but other stereotypes can be just as harmful. Broadening teacher training beyond teaching is called for.

The other policy direction is to help low achievers who have not benefited from smaller classes and the other educational innovations of the last two decades. If enough first rate teachers are available, perhaps more can finally be persuaded to teach in the schools that need them most. Also, every child is entitled to the educational assistance that many upper middle and middle class children receive at home both before they start school and after their school years have begun. Whether that entitlement can be realized by helping parents or through changes in the schools requires testing.

Traditionally, parents who never received home preschooling themselves have had the greatest difficulty supplying it to their children. If the parents of these parents were in the same boat, the problem is as multigenerational as the country's slowness in reducing economic and social inequality.

As America moves toward greater economic equality, more parents will be able to break the generational cycle by themselves. Even so, the schools must figure out how they can help parents or provide a school-based substitute for the home learning process.

Nonetheless, the country and the White House may face a much bigger challenge: the impact of the emerging economy and its changing labor market conditions on student educational incentives. The Council knows that in the foreseeable future, economic growth and the global economic competition will require a continuing increase in highly skilled workers. The Council also believes that the educational reforms of the last generation, in public and higher education, will produce the needed workers.

Consequently, the Council is concerned with the workers who will take up the less skilled and semiskilled jobs so abundant in the broad array of "service" industries. At some point, the government may have to decide how much and what kind of career oriented assistance it will choose to offer them.

More important, educational policymakers and others must ask how much and what kind of education students will be willing to accept. Moreover, if a decline in work hours takes place, and if the workers in less skilled and semiskilled service jobs are likely to face the brunt of the work hours decline, their children and other young people will eventually ask themselves why they should perform well in school. Students for whom such performance is hard work might decide to stop trying to learn.

The pattern is not new, for poor children have often tuned out or dropped out of school because occupational and other payoffs seem unlikely. If more children are driven toward this pattern, however, educators will have to come up with alternative payoffs that would motivate young people. Educational innovation may have to start nearly from scratch.

Furthermore, the Council expects that, if the past is any guide, some critics, many of them well educated Americans, will ask how their fellow Americans will spend the free time that comes with reduced work hours. Others might follow up the utopian criticism of the Community Service Work Program [described at the close of chap. 2, "Healing the Economy"]. They will suggest that periods of work time reduction offer the opportunity for more Americans to pursue intellectual, artistic, and other cultural activities that they claim are, to use a recently popular phrase, hardwired into their genetic makeup.

These critics will probably be joined by a larger set of dystopian critics who will worry once more that, when work is scarce, bored people will either amuse themselves to death with entertainment or cure their boredom with drugs and alcohol. Many more forms of "soma" than the twentieth-century novelist Aldous Huxley could have imagined have already been available for a long time, yet the number of Americans seeking oblivion through hard drugs has remained small and stable.

The Council believes that both the utopian and the dystopian scenarios lack credibility. Perhaps the economy will someday have to cope with drastic reductions of work time or jobs, but then Americans will be busy creating new ways of working to make money before they invent new leisure pursuits and recreational activities.

A CAVEAT

The Council of Long-Range Advisers voted to conclude its report by suggesting that the predictive and policy-oriented planning with which it is charged bears some resemblance to baseball. Like baseball coaches, policy analysts can chart and project trends, but even so, neither can ever predict what will happen in the next inning.